Landscapes and Gardens of Auroville

the transformation of the land

Copyright: Prisma, Auroville
Author: Franz Fassbender
Photographs: John Mandeen

First edition: 2013

ISBN: 978-93-95460-26-2 (Paperpack)
ISBN: 978-93-95460-23-1 (ebook)

BISAC Code:
ARC008000 ARCHITECTURE / Landscape
ARC005000, ARCHITECTURE / History / General
ARC007000, ARCHITECTURE / Interior Design / General
ARC015000, ARCHITECTURE / Professional Practice
ARC012000, ARCHITECTURE / Reference
ARC020000, ARCHITECTURE / Regional
ARC013000, ARCHITECTURE / Study & Teaching
ARC025000, ARCHITECTURE / Vernacular

Thema Subject Category:
AMV, Landscape architecture and design
AMA, Theory of architecture
AMR, Architecture: interior design
AMX, History of architecture
AMCR, Environmentally-friendly ('green') architecture and design
AMD, Architecture: professional practice
WJK, Interior design, decor and style guides

Cataloging-in-Publication Data for this title is available from the Library of Congress.

Digital Editions produced by:
DMI Systems Pvt Ltd, Vishnupuri,
Aligarh 202001, Uttar Pradesh, India
www.dmi.systems

Published by:
PRISMA, Aurelec/ Prayogshala, Auroville 605101,
Tamil Nadu, India
www.prisma.haus

ACKNOWLEDGEMENTS

The texts by Sri Aurobindo and the Mother are copyright of the Sri Aurobindo Ashram Trust, Pondicherry, and are reproduced here with acknowledgement and thanks to the Trustees. The copyright holder for Mother's Agenda is "Institut de Recherches Evolutives", Paris.

Contents

I invite you to the great adventure

Well, I announced to you all that this new world was born. But it has been so engulfed, as it were, in the old world that so far the difference has not been very perceptible to many people. Still, the action of the new forces has continued very regularly, very persistently, very steadily, and to a certain extent, very effectively.

And one of the manifestations of this action was my experience – truly so very new – of yesterday evening. And the result of all this I have noted step by step in almost daily experiences. It could be expressed succinctly, in a rather linear way.

First, it is not only a "new conception" of spiritual life and the divine Reality. This conception was expressed by Sri Aurobindo, I have expressed it myself many a time, and it could be formulated somewhat like this: the old spirituality was an escape from life into the divine Reality, leaving the world just where it was, as it was; whereas our new vision, on the contrary, is a divinisation of life, a transformation of the material world into a divine world. This has been said, repeated, more or less understood, indeed it is the basic idea of what we want to do. But this could be a continuation with an improvement, a widening of the old world as it was – and so long as this is a conception up there in the field of thought, in fact it is hardly more than that – but what has happened, the really new thing, is that a new world is born, born, born. It is not the old one transforming itself, it is a new world which is born. And we are right in the midst of this period of transition where the two are entangled – where the other still persists all-powerful and entirely dominating the ordinary consciousness, but where the new one is quietly slipping in, still very modest, unnoticed – unnoticed to the extent that outwardly it doesn't disturb anything very much, for the time being, and that in the consciousness of most people it is even altogether imperceptible. And yet it is working, growing – until it is strong enough to assert itself visibly.

In any case, to simplify things, it could be said that characteristically the old world, the creation of what Sri Aurobindo calls the Overmind, was an age of the gods, and consequently the age of religions. As I said, the flower of human effort towards what is above it gave rise to innumerable religious forms, to a religious relationship between the best souls and the invisible world. And at the very summit of all that, as an effort towards a higher realization, there has arisen the idea of the unity of religions, of this "one single thing" which is behind all these manifestations; and this idea has truly been, so to speak, the extreme limit of human aspiration. Well, that is at the frontier, it is something that still belongs completely to the Overmind world, the Overmind creation, and which from there seems to be looking towards this "other thing" which is a new creation it cannot grasp – which it tries to reach, feels coming, but cannot grasp. To grasp it, a reversal is needed. It is necessary to leave the Overmind creation. It was necessary that the new creation, the supramental creation should take place.

And now, all these old things seem so old, so out-of-date, so arbitrary – such a travesty of the real truth. In the supramental creation there will no longer be any religions. The whole life will be the expression, the flowering into forms of the divine Unity manifesting in the world. And there will no longer be what men now call gods.

These great divine beings themselves will be able to participate in the new creation; but to do so, they will have to put on what we could call the "supramental substance" on earth. And if some of them choose to remain in their world as they are, if they decide not to manifest physically, their relation with the beings of a supramental earth will be a relation of friends, collaborators, equals, for the highest divine essence will be manifested in the beings of the new supramental world on earth.

When the physical substance is supramentalised, to incarnate on earth will no longer be a cause of inferiority, quite the contrary. It will give a plenitude which cannot be obtained otherwise.

But all this is in the future; it is a future... which has begun, but which will take some time to be realised integrally. Meanwhile we are in a very special situation, extremely special, without precedent. We are now witnessing the birth of a new world; it is very young, very weak – not in its essence but in its outer manifestation – not yet recognised, not even felt, denied by the majority. But it is here. It is here, making an effort to grow, absolutely sure of the result. But the road to it is a completely new road which has never before been traced out – nobody has gone there, nobody has done that! It is a beginning, a universal beginning.

So, it is an absolutely unexpected and unpredictable adventure.

There are people who love adventure. It is these I call, and I tell them this: "I invite you to the great adventure."

It is not a question of repeating spiritually what others have done before us, for our adventure begins beyond that. It is a question of a new creation, entirely new, with all the unforeseen events, the risks, the hazards it entails – a real adventure, whose goal is certain victory, but the road to which is unknown and must be traced out step by step in the unexplored. Something that has never been in this present universe and that will never be again in the same way. If that interests you... well, let us embark. What will happen to you tomorrow – I have no idea.

One must put aside all that has been foreseen, all that has been devised, all that has been constructed, and then... set off walking into the unknown.

And – come what may! There.

The Mother

A lonely Palmyra tree, a sandy road, and behind an almost bare landscape.

In the beginning there was nothing

The land was so poor it could barely sustain life; almost all the local villagers were hungry. Poor agricultural practices together with over-grazing had left a windswept barren plateau that UNESCO said would be unable to support human life within twenty years.

There were dust storms during the summer, when there was nothing to hold the little topsoil in place, composed of a fine red sand-like substance that had the insidious ability to penetrate everything, everywhere; nothing was spared. After having our brains baked for six months the monsoon would set in, in October. Over 80% of the rainwater would flow into the canyons and ravines for its trip to the sea, and the flood of rainwater would sweep yet more of the little remaining topsoil into the sea. The Bay of Bengal would appear red for kilometres from the shore after a heavy rain. Without the topsoil, the clay base hardpan alone could not absorb the rainwater. When we tried to plough the land, in places it was so hard the plough would bounce off the surface, unable to penetrate the earth. The absence of borewells in the villages made all life there depend on the rains. When the tropical monsoon rain arrived the erosion multiplied. In 1969 the monsoon failed almost completely. All the water tanks in all the surrounding villages went dry. We spent our time getting water on to bullock carts and into as many villages as possible from the few borewells Auroville had at the time. Our pumps worked from dawn to dusk.

It did not take an Einstein to understand what had to be done.

The Success Tree Nursery was started with the Mother's blessings. The Sri Aurobindo Ashram School children would come out to Auroville and help us collect seeds and fill plastic bags for the seedlings. Whole villages were hired to dig holes for the tree seedlings or to make bunds in an attempt to keep the rainwater on the land, and prevent it from reaching the sea. Overnight we became the largest employer in the area. Men worked for two rupees a day, women for one rupee, and petrol was one rupee a litre.

Local landowners complained that we were paying the workers too much and not working them hard enough.

We were told that we were upsetting the balance that had been in place for hundreds of years. For the first time in their lives young men had money in their pockets, and village life would never be the same again.

We all lived in keet- or wallha-roofed huts with mud walls and cow dung floors. A millet mix of fermented ragi and kambu was our staple food. With joy in our hearts, continually sunburnt, and infested with intestinal parasites, no one questioned why we were involved in this insane project, on this dying land, for we were all high on the Mother's energy.

Protecting the seedlings from the village women and from goats and cows was a major task. After all the work that it would take to get a tree seedling in place, a village woman searching for firewood would take it out with a single swing of her knife, or a goat would tear it in half with a quick twist of its mouth.

During the hot dry summer months, bullock carts would carry large drums of water. These would fill large clay jars that women would carry, and they would give a few litres of water to each and every seedling of the thousands upon thousands that we planted.

For the first four years that was the main work, and then we started organizing schools and digging the foundations of the Matrimandir.

Francis

Auroville located in Tamil Nadu

Auroville, which is located in Tamil Nadu, close to the Coromandel Coast, was started in 1968. As a physical entity it is planned to be only around 5 kms in diameter inclusive of a surrounding Green Belt. Back in 1968, the land was already denuded of nearly all vegetation, and frequent dust storms and monsoon deluges stripped it further of its meagre topsoil, carving ravines as rainwater poured down from the plateau into the sea. The local villagers were living in small palm-leaf thatched huts, and in some families the women could

The Auroville landscape – early days.

come out only one at a time because there was only one saree to wear between them. In some villages they had to walk 2 kms to fetch water. Most were eating only a gruel made of the millets which they were growing on their infertile fields, and they were looking malnourished. But they had hope. Many responded to the call of the Mother to sell their lands to Auroville, and they were eager to work, which they were able to do even in the hot sun. They were also ready to learn new skills, a new language, new ways of living.

Herdsmen and children guiding cows and goats through the canyon landscape of early Auroville. Palmyra trees were the first and virtually only trees in the barren landscape.

Historical aspects of Auroville

Although Auroville is a township under construction, the landscape in which it is situated has already had countless previous incarnations and avatars. Of special interest to Aurovilians is the fact that a few kilometres away is its 'mother-town', Pondicherry, the home of Sri Aurobindo and the Mother, the site of the Sri Aurobindo Ashram.

The origins of Pondicherry go back to the mists of time. The original name of the town, no longer used, was Vedapuri, and a big temple still stands today, the Vedapurishwara temple, dedicated to the great god Siva, the god of the contemplatives. Vedapuri means 'city of knowledge'. The patron saint of Vedapuri was Sri Agastya, who according to legend came from the far Himalayas, travelling south, to settle in the country of the

Wooden bullock carts were the only vehicles of transport in those early days.

Tamils and teach the people the Veda. For thousands of years, Vedapuri was a school for young Brahmins where they learned to chant the Vedic hymns in Sanskrit and to perform complicated rituals in the proper way.

Buddhism came and went, and then in the first and second centuries of our era we find on that same Coromandel Coast a Roman settlement mentioned in the *Periple* by Ptolemy of Alexandria. Heavily loaded ships came from the far Mediterranean, swept by the constant trade winds, to arrive via Cleopatra's Nile–Red Sea Canal at Poduke, as our town was then called. It was a Roman emporium, a trader's town where Mediterranean wines and swords, Germanic slaves and Roman gold were exchanged for the spices and silks, precious stones, cottons and peacocks of India. The poet-prince Ilango, brother of the Chera king

Granite stone markers were used to define Auroville areas of land.

Kovalan, describes how – like some future Auroville – it appeared in the first century in the following text, which is translated from the original picturesque Tamil.

"The sun shone over the open terraces, over the warehouses near the harbour, and over the turrets with their air-holes like the eyes of the deer (a description of windows built with a Roman arch). In different places the observer's attention was arrested by the sight of Yavanas (a name for Greeks and Romans) whose prosperity never waned.

"In the harbour were to be seen sailing vessels with many sailors from distant lands. To all appearances they lived as one community. In the streets of the city hawkers went about with cosmetics, bath powders, cool pastes, flowers, incense and fragrant perfumes. In certain places weavers were seen dealing in fine fabrics of silk, animal hair and cotton. Whole streets were full of cloth, corals, sandalwood and myrrh, besides a wealth of rare ornaments, perfect pearls, gems and gold beyond all reckoning."

Children make their way across a stark open landscape

The description of the city itself and the central highway leading to it also has its poetic charm: "Entering into the central highway of the city, rich with the wealth of sea-borne goods and reaching down to the seashore where flags of foreign countries fly high, one is impressed by these stretches of white sand where are displayed various kinds of goods brought in by ships of foreign merchants who have left their homes and settled here.

"Here, burning in the evening, were myriads of lamps: lamps of those who sold coloured powders, who sold sandalwood, jasmine flowers, scents, and all varieties of sweets; the lamps of dexterous goldsmiths, and of those who, sitting in a row, sold pittu; the broad black lamps placed on lampstands by the sellers of muffins; the lamps of fishmongers glimmering here and there; and high above all the bright beacon lights erected to guide ships to the shore.

There were lamps taken out to sea by fishermen in their boats as they went with their nets, night-long lights set out by foreigners speaking strange languages, and

A portion of the road from Aspiration down to the coast road.

finally the lamps lit by the watchmen of the warehouses containing valuable merchandise from far away countries."

Recent archaeological excavations of a low hill called Arikamedu south of Pondicherry have yielded Greek and Roman coins and imported Mediterranean pottery, reminiscent of a trade very much to the detriment of the Roman empire.

Such was the eagerness of Roman ladies to possess the colourful silks and fine muslins of India that Rome lost much of its gold reserves in this exchange, but it benefited the kings of the Coromandel Coast, who became fabulously rich and were able to build the huge temple towns of Rameswaram and Chidambaram, of Madurai and Trichinopoly, and – less than a hundred miles from where Auroville is being built – the magnificent Versailles of India, Mahabalipuram.

A lone woman heads home down an eroded earth road.

Vedapuri itself fell asleep. The destructive force of Islam came and went; the Portuguese came and called the town 'Puducheira', and the Dutch 'Poeleser', and the Danes – all trying to get some of the gold the Romans had lost – and built their trading posts, their 'comptoirs'. In the 17th century came the French, who built on the shore the largest and most powerful fortress in southern India. As a fortress it was very successful; also as a safe place for investments in gold during troubled times. It quickly became rich, too rich for the jealous British in Madras, who razed it to the ground.

Rebuilt in the 18th century in the French provincial style, the town could be seen from the plateau of Auroville, now a part of free India.

Only a few small fishermen's villages without history stand today where the 20th century, with its big bulldozers, is moving in to build the city of a new dawn.

Equals One

Another view of the road opposite, showing the severity of the erosion from unchecked run-off.

Buses and cars driving
on sandy roads
to Auroville's inauguration.

Inauguration of Auroville 28 February 1968

CAMBODIA
BURMA
CU
BURMA
BULGARIA
BOLIVIA

The inauguration day, February 28, 1968

The delegates, young people from India and abroad, boarded the buses, four or five buses with hundreds of people. People came from the Sri Aurobindo Ashram, from all the Indian states and foreign countries, from all the villages around. Buses, cars and many bicycles.

From Jipmer hospital onwards there was nothing: a desert. Edayanchavadi was a sleepy village of mud huts. Only peanut fields, a few palmyra trees growing here and there in line, and not so many. One could see everything from here down to Pondicherry. Then the buses stopped in the middle of nowhere and everybody got out. It was about

10 a.m., but already very hot. Shades were put up and the delegates had to wait there. The atmosphere was vibrating. One could feel the enormity of the event, it was the human unity, the international atmosphere, like what you may feel in the Olympic Games, but there it is very much vital, while here it was bright, it was of another quality.

All the delegates, in alphabetical order, one by one had to go to the urn in the middle of an upcoming amphitheatre and place soil of their country in the urn. Then they had to sign a scroll.

The Auroville Charter was read out in many languages.

The Mother on Auroville

Then I have written something else....They wanted to prepare a sort of brochure on Auroville to distribute to the press, the government, etc, on the 28th, and before that there is in Delhi in two or three days a conference of all nations...

So then I asked, I concentrated to know what had to be said. And all of a sudden, Sri Aurobindo gave me a revelation. That was something interesting. I concentrated to know the why, the how and so on, and all of a sudden Sri Aurobindo said ... (Mother reads out a note.)

"India has become...
It was the vision of the thing, and it instantly translated into French words

India has become the symbolic representation of all the difficulties of modern mankind.
India will be the land of its resurrection – the resurrection to a higher and truer life."

And the clear vision: the same thing which in the history of the universe made the earth the symbolic representation of the universe so as to concentrate the work on one point, the same phenomenon is now taking place: India is the representation of all human difficulties on earth, and it is in India that the . . . cure will be found. And then, that is why – **THAT IS WHY** I was made to start Auroville.

It came and it was so clear, so tremendously powerful! It was very interesting. It remained the whole time, for more than an hour, such a strong and clear vision, as if suddenly everything became clear. I often used to wonder about it (not "wonder," but there was a tension to understand why things, here in India, have become such a chaos, with such sordid difficulties, and all of it piling up), and instantly, everything became clear, like that. It was really interesting. And immediately there was: "Here is why you have made Auroville.

I didn't know it, you understand, I did the thing under pressure, and it took larger and larger proportions (it's becoming really worldwide), and I would wonder why. . . For a time I thought it was the only present possibility to prevent a war, but it seemed to me a somewhat superficial explanation. Then it came all of a sudden: "Ah! That's why.

And as that whole power was in it, I said, "Put it." We'll see – they won't understand anything, but that doesn't matter, it will act.

Mother's Agenda

Auroville's Charter

1. **Auroville belongs to nobody in particular. Auroville belongs to humanity as a whole.
    But to live in Auroville one must be a willing servitor of the Divine Consciousness.**

2. **Auroville will be the place of an unending education, of constant progress, and a youth that never ages.**

3. **Auroville wants to be the bridge between the past and the future. Taking advantage of all discoveries from without and from within, Auroville will boldly spring towards future realisations.**

4. **Auroville will be a site of material and spiritual researches for a living embodiment of an actual Human Unity.**

(then the microphone is switched off. . . silence)

The inaugural event

The entire Ashram has gone to Auroville to attend its inauguration. The ceremony, which would take 75 minutes, began at 10.24 with the white-clad announcer briefly explaining the order of events to come to the 5,000 or so people assembled in the amphitheatre. At 10.30 there was the sound of a gong, there were a few bars of Mother's music, then came Mother's voice, relayed from her room in the Ashram: Mother reads out her message, which is broadcast live to Auroville through All India Radio:

Salut d'Auroville à tous les hommes de bonne volonté. Sont conviés à Auroville tous ceux qui ont soif de progrès et aspirent à une vie plus haute et plus vraie.

Greetings from Auroville to all men of good will. Are invited to Auroville all those who thirst for progress and aspire to a higher and truer life.

A few more bars of music followed, then Mother read The Charter of Auroville in French.

The announcer then stated, "Now the earth from the Ashram will be put in the urn." Kiran and Vijay Poddar approached the urn. Kiran carried Mother's flag and Vijay carried earth from the Samadhi and a stainless steel container with inside the scroll with The Charter of Auroville in Mother's handwriting. As they reached the urn Sunil's 1968 New Year music began to be played, along with Mother's New Year message: "Remain young, Never stop striving towards Perfection." The stainless steel container was lowered deep into the urn using ribbons, along with the earth.

The announcer then introduced the formula which would be followed for the rest of the ceremony. The Charter would be read successively in 16 languages by nationals (usually Ashramites) of those countries or cultures (the languages in order were Tamil, Sanskrit, English, Arabic, Chinese, Dutch, German, Greek, Hebrew, Italian, Japanese, Norwegian, Russian, Spanish, Swedish and Tibetan). Before each reading the announcer would introduce the translation — "Now the Charter in Tamil will be read..." — and specify which states of India or countries would approach the urn during that reading (the states first, countries afterwards, all in alphabetical order). In all, two young delegates from each of the 23 States or Union Territories of India and representatives from 124 countries (63 persons were delegated by embassies, the rest were students from the Ashram school) walked up to the urn. In each pair one would carry a placard with the name of their State or country, the other would carry earth (or a substitute) from that State or country in a small bowl. After the earth was tipped into the urn, the representatives walked down the ramp from the urn. Their placard was taken and placed in a pre-assigned socket, they signed a scroll with their names and the name of their State or country, and then they walked up a ramp out of the central arena.

Finally came the announcement, "Now the earth of Auroville will be put in the urn. Then the urn will be sealed." Michel (Kalya) and Fabienne, Mother' s great-grandchildren, approached the urn. Michel carried Auroville earth while Fabienne carried the Auroville flag (the symbol was an open lotus with another lotus in its centre against a background of 'dawn gold'). Then Nolini and his son walked to the urn. He placed the lid over the top and removed the screwed handle. The urn was sealed, the inauguration of Auroville complete.

February 28, 1968

Nolinida, Mother's secretary and also secretary of the Sri Aurobindo Ashram, seals the urn that will be at the heart of the Auroville amphitheatre.

The Banyan tree, geographical centre of Auroville, ▶ is a sacred tree - Ficus religiosa - symbol of paradise and of creation, of life and illumination.

The Mother on preparation for February 28, 1968

I've spent all my days and all my nights quieting the atmosphere, it had taken such proportions . . . You know, those movements which start whirling like that, like the wind in a cyclone or at sea, and it goes on whirling faster and faster, more and more strongly and forcefully. Then people fall ill, they get worn out, they can't do anything anymore. For the past three days I've spent my time calming and calming the atmosphere. Luckily they came to me (it wasn't to "me," naturally), they felt there was something stable here that could stop this disorder, otherwise. . . But it was very difficult because of the really large number of additions from outside: on the 21st, at the Darshan, they were more than four thousand people down in the street, and there are all those who came to be here today and tomorrow, so it must mean five or six thousand people to feed, accommodate . . . a whole work.

Then they asked me, naturally, that it shouldn't rain, but that it shouldn't be sunny either! (Mother laughs) So it was a bit difficult, but a short while ago, Z came to tell me that Auroville's area was clouded, without sunshine... All these little entities are quite obliging, but they're asked impossible things! I get requests, "Ah, I need rain," and at the same time, "Oh, no, I don't want rain"; "Ah, I need sunshine," and "Oh, no, I don't want sunshine..." How can they manage it?

Mother's Agenda

Conversation between Mother and a disciple about Auroville on February 28, 1968

One needs to have an absolutely transparent sincerity. Lack of sincerity is at present the cause of difficulties.

Insincerity is in all men. There are perhaps a hundred totally sincere men on earth. Man's very nature is what makes him insincere. It's very complicated, for he is constantly cheating with himself, hiding the truth from himself, finding excuses for himself. Yoga is the way to become sincere in all the parts of one's being.

It is difficult to be sincere, but one can at least be mentally sincere – this is what one can demand from Aurovilians.

The Force is there, present as never before; what prevents it from descending and being felt is men's insincerity. The world is steeped in falsehood, all relationships between men have so far been based only on falsehood and deceit. Diplomacy between nations is based on falsehood. They claim they want peace and on the other hand arm themselves. A transparent sincerity in man and between nations will alone permit the coming of a transformed world.

Auroville is the first attempt in the experiment. A new world will be born if men consent to strive for transformation and the search for sincerity – it can be done. It took millennia to evolve from animal to man; today man, thanks to his mind, can accelerate things and will a transformation towards a man who will be God.

This transformation with the help of the mind, through self-analysis, is a first stage; afterwards, vital impulses must be transformed – which is far more difficult; then, most of all, the physical: each cell of our body will have to become conscious. It is the work I am doing here. It will allow the conquest of death. It's another story; that will be future mankind, perhaps in centuries, perhaps sooner. It will depend on men, on peoples.

Auroville is the first step towards this goal.
Mother's Agenda

The Banyan tree
is festively decorated
for Auroville's inauguration day.

Ancient site

Not long after Auroville started Aurovilians began studying the history of the area – to find out if, when and why the trees had all been cut. They did research in the French Institute in Pondicherry, where they found many treatises written by colonial scholars over the past centuries. In course of their studies they found evidence in ancient texts that it really was true that some 250 years ago the land on which Auroville is sited had been a dense forest, with elephants and tigers. There had been a kingdom in the area, of which the Irumbai temple and name "Kottakarai" (corner of the fort) village are remnants. But there was little left to reflect those past glories, although the digging of pits in the soil for tree planting unearthed a number of ancient burial grounds that archaeological experts dated back to 2,000 years ago, and indicated a trade with Rome.

We find megalithic burial-grounds, mostly in the form of stone circles in Auroville in the area between Bharat Nivas and Matrimandir. They date from 1,000 B.C. to 300 A.D. a period of post-Vedic civilizations, the Mauryan empire, Alexander of Macedonia. There are huge boulders placed in a circle, a cairn circle, large granite slabs covering urns underground or capstone burials, boulders or slabs supporting a ceiling slab stone or dolmens.

Excavation between Bharat Nivas and Matrimandir, March 2013

Excavation of a megalithic Cairn Circle, 1987-88

AUROVILLE: the city with the built-in revolution

Once we realize that we are living in an evolutionary universe, in which evolution means continuous change and rapid evolution means revolution, we have to welcome revolution rather than resist it.

We should organize it so that it becomes permanent and can be directed into constructive, creative channels instead of destructive ones.

The great revolutions are political only on the surface, in the froth; below, they are technological. And behind the technological upheavals, behind the commotion, there is a new insight into the mystery of the universe, and ahead a wider consciousness for man. A hidden spiritual intention is there in every revolution.

In the new city we will accept rather than resist experimentation, and salute as the outer sign of a breakthrough into new fields of spiritual endeavour each new invention which changes our society. A continuous spiritual adventure we will now recognize as the chief raison d'être of the human race, and its only justification for violating the old equilibriums of nature.

The general unrest which we observe around us, in every country regardless of its political regime, in all classes of society and all races, and especially in the younger generation, has a deeper meaning than we generally suspect. It is the sign of a spiritual upheaval, of a sudden mutation of the race.

In the next hundred years our planet will have changed so much that one could call it an entirely different planet.

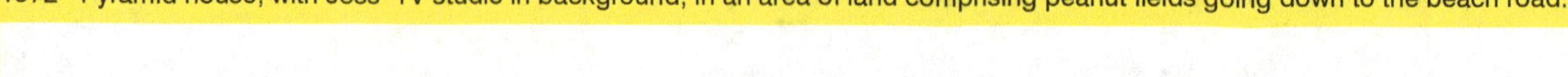

1972 - Pyramid house, with Joss' TV studio in background, in an area of land comprising peanut fields going down to the beach road.

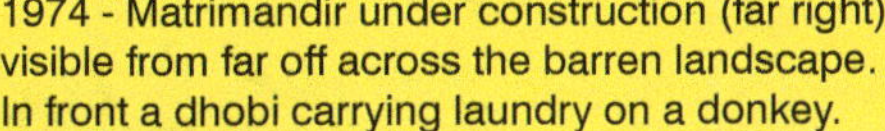
1974 - Matrimandir under construction (far right),
visible from far off across the barren landscape.
In front a dhobi carrying laundry on a donkey.

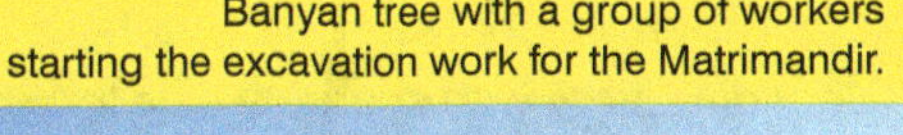
Banyan tree with a group of workers
starting the excavation work for the Matrimandir.

None of our nations, none of our educational institutions, none of our ancient values will survive. In a hundred year's time all our literature and most of our languages will have disappeared.

In comparison with the time we live in, the past 10,000 years of man's history constituted a slow and almost steady evolution of social formations and sacred institutions. There was comfortable and easily understandable continuity in art and weaponry, in philosophy and technology, from the prehistoric paintings in Altamira and Lascaux to Rembrandt and Rubens and Monet; a straight line from the stone axe to the spear to the musket, from the Veda to the epics, to Hegel and Marx and Schopenhauer, from prehistoric buildings to the skyscrapers.

But then comes a clean cut: Picasso, Pollock, electronic music, and the mathematics of Cantor; the laser, communication satellites, spaceships. And this cut is irreversible. We are no longer living at the tired end of an age, but at the very beginning of a new one. All around us are entirely new things like unlimited atomic power, unlimited mind power (computers), unlimited life power (biogenetic engineering), unlimited frontiers in space.

Each of these things would be sufficient in itself to usher in a new age.

We are not riding any longer in the oxcart of history, we are in orbit.

Every few years our knowledge doubles. The books we print are out of date before they reach the shelves. We spend most of our time unlearning what we have learned and trying to get rid of our old opinions. Whatever we organize will be obsolete by the time it is done.

The most obsolete things around us are our political institutions, our barbarian economic systems with their gold and paper money and banks, the division of our planet into nations, into east and west, capitalism and communism, when both are already long gone. While weaponry had always first priority of access to men's highest capabilities, city building, with the exception of a few prestige capitals, has always been in the lowest priority area.

Whatever we do in Auroville as we experiment with new forms of society and new economic systems, we will be conscious precursors of the great geosocial revolution. We will dedicate ourselves to the ushering in of the new age, the spiritual age.

Equals One

First years

Auroville was started in I968, it was hardly a welcoming
scene: barren dry red soil stretching to the horizon in
every direction, with scarcely a tree to stand under. Well,
there was one forlorn banyan looking rather uncertain
of itself, under which was living an old woman who
provided water to foot travellers from the inland villages
on their way to Pondicherry. She was the one who first
shared the tale of Kaluveli Siddha, the ancient legend
which predicted that in a distant future "people from far
away" would come to transform the cursed wasteland
into a beautiful green area.

Early landscape with Aspiration community in the foreground, on the horizon Pondicherry. Only a few trees and nothing else until Kottakuppam, Muthialpet and Pondicherry town.

Child goatherds near the future Amphitheatre and on the road to Aspiration

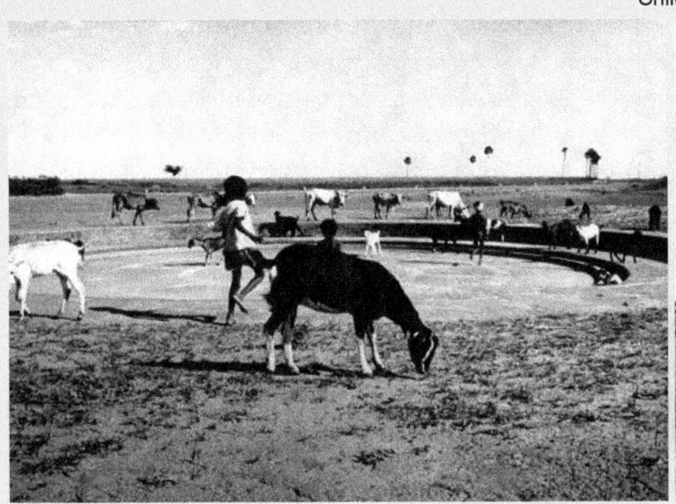

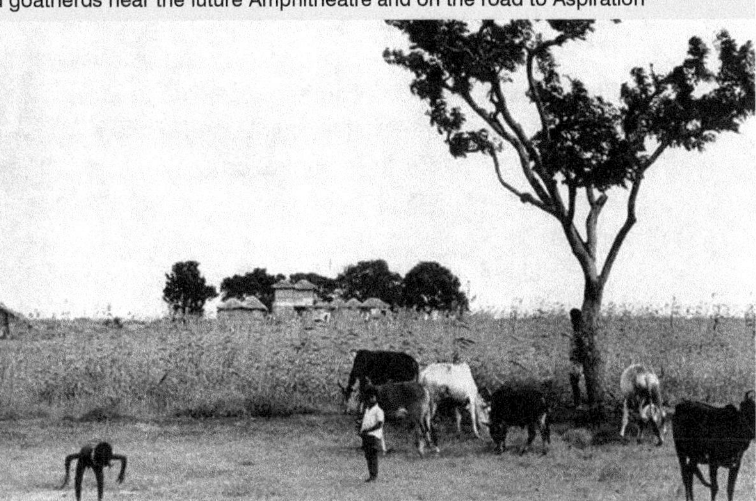

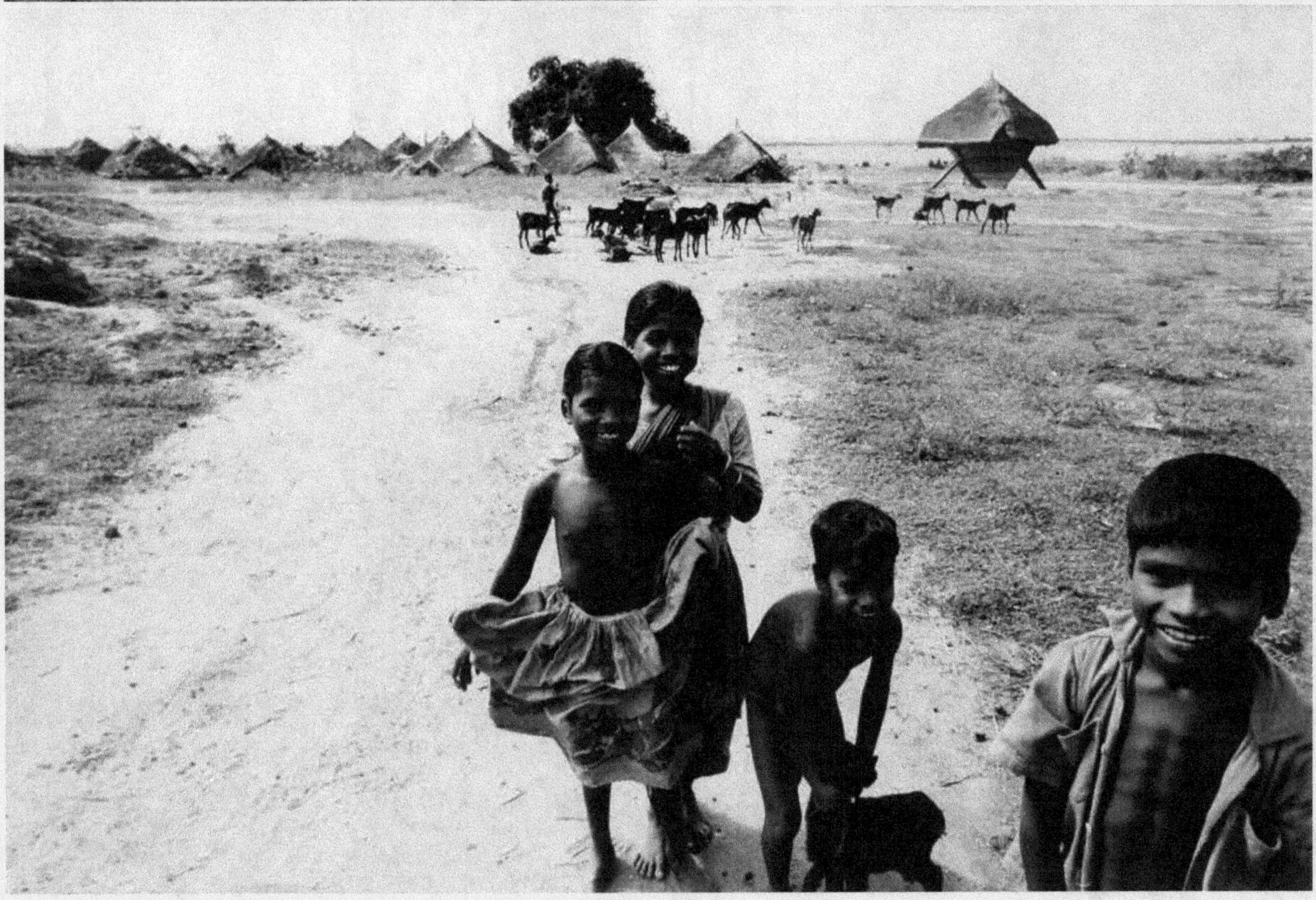

Legend of Irumbai Temple

Wandering the barren canyon lands of Auroville or down the dusty village roads past crumbling temple ghats, one cannot help but wonder about an ancient culture that outwardly has been relegated to ruin, yet inwardly still haunts us with a hidden sense of epic grandeur and of might. Who were the priests, saints and rishis of these temples? What were their aspirations? What were the stories and traditions of these villages we pass through every day?

Our daily contacts with the villages through work, through disputes over land and grazing rights, through brief glimpses caught as one passes by, of temples, of crowds in the evening dusk, of people staring silently, of tea-shops and low dark huts, gives one the strange impression of two cultures hurled together to find something, at what is, perhaps, the end of an Age.

The villages of Irumbai, Kottakarai, and Edayanchavadi, sites of continual daily contact between Auroville and the Tamil reality, have temple traditions going back millennia. They tend to show a strong devotion to the god Shiva, and among their stories and traditions, Auroville, as the legend of Kaduveli and temple of Irumbai will show, is not absent.

The temple of Irumbai represents an important cultural and historical site, its sanctum sanctorum dating back more than 2,000 years. It is mentioned in the collection of songs called the "Thevaram" of the famous Shaivite saint of the South, Thirugnana Sambanthar, who lived some twelve to fourteen hundred years ago, and who composed songs on the presiding deities and the geographical locality of almost all the early Shiva temples in the

Planting of the first trees in Aurogreen.

South. He sang of the presiding deity of Irumbai temple, Mahakaleswara, as well as the goddess Kuilmorhli Ammai, which means: "Mother with the sweet voice of the kuyil birds." He depicts the Irumbai temple and its surroundings in beautiful language, mentioning the lotus pond, the green fields around the temple, and the thick forests surrounding Irumbai village, which are today non-existent.

The temple was renovated under the Cholas and the Pandyas, whose kings donated hundreds of acres of land to the temple, and it had at one point perhaps as many as seven outer walls. A large statue of the god Ganesh, once part of the temple, now stands in the village itself.

Today, the temple sits at the entrance of Irumbai village beside the large crumbling stones of the lotus pond ghat where villagers bathe in the lazy afternoon, and despite its urgent need of repairs, still commands that ancient sense of power which in India overrides the ruins and ravages of time. It is the courtyard of the first of the seven walls that still exists, and stands facing the west pillar of the Matrimandir across the rice paddies a couple of kilometres away.

The temple is particularly associated with the legend of Kaduveli Siddha, a famous yogi who lived in the area some four to five hundred years ago. He is remembered for his songs on how to control one's anger (Ref: "Songs of the Siddhas" in Tamil), and his wooden Samadhi is to be found on the road from Edayanchavadi to Pondy, close to the community of Forecomers. It is around him that the legend of Irumbai temple is based.

According to the legend, Kaduveli Siddha was performing a harsh penance. Sitting under a peepal tree in yogic poise for days on end, the heat of his body

was so intense that the rain Gods suffered; no rains came, and the people were exposed to hardship and drought. The situation was so bad that it finally came to the ears of the King, who ruled from Edayanchavadi village, the region of which Irumbai was an important cultural centre. Kottakarai, today a village adjoining the Auroville settlement of the same name, was one of his forts (Kottakarai in fact means "End of the fort").

No-one dared disturb Kaduveli in his penance as he chanted the mantra of Eswara, and soon an anthill started to rise up around him. Finally a temple dancer, named Valli, devoted to the Lord Shiva, decided to do her best to get the attention of the yogi, and to rescue the King and his people from the adverse effects of his tapasya. She observed that occasionally the Siddha would, with his eyes shut, put out his hands to catch and consume the falling, withered peepal leaves. So she prepared some thinly fried apalam (a flat salty wafer made out of green gram dhal) and started placing them into the yogi's outstretched hands as he sought to catch the falling leaves. Soon he started eating the apalams and getting his taste back. As he did so he grew fatter, until finally the anthill broke and fell, and he was once more exposed to the rays of the sun. Finally he opened his eyes. Valli was extremely happy, and was able to take him back to her house, where she kept him in the best of moods by dancing for him, at the same time learning songs from him. Meanwhile the God of Rain was relieved from the torture induced on him by the heat of the yogi's tapasya, and the rain fell in plenty, making the people happy once again.

In order to celebrate this event the King ordered a big Puja to be held at Irumbai temple, which was to be

followed by a classical performance by Valli of one of the highest orders of dance, in which she would act out the cosmic dance of Lord Shiva, in the form of Nataraja. During the performance, however, one of her anklets fell off, and she started suddenly to lose her balance and rhythm. Kaduveli, who saw the Lord Shiva in Valli, picked up the anklet and put it back on her foot. This exposed him to the ridicule of King and court for having touched the feet of a dancing girl, and he was heckled and jeered. Furious, he invoked Lord Shiva to come out of his temple and prove his innocence in a rain of stone. Immediately the lingam in the sanctum sanctorum of the temple exploded, and wherever its fragments fell suddenly became desert. No greenery will grow around these spots, including a crater at a distance of three kilometres from the village, and they are still to this day known as 'Kaduveli'.

The King was suddenly frightened and begged the pardon of the Siddha, bowing down to him with all his entourage and pleading with him to quench the effects of his anger and curse. This appeased Kaduveli, who, repenting of his anger, said that what was done was done and could not be undone, but that in the future people from far-off lands would come and make the desert land green and fertile again. Today there are villagers who feel that the Aurovilians are the people from far-off lands mentioned by the Siddha and that the curse is now beginning to leave them.

Whatever one's interpretation of the legend might be, it is in any case an interesting tale, and the next time one passes through what was once the kingdom of Edayanchavadi, one might well wonder about this story of the dancer, the Siddha, and the people from far-off lands, that occurred some five hundred years ago.

A stone with an AV sign marks a corner of Auroville land.

Real people

Of course, it is unknown if Aurovilians were destined to be the prophesied redeemers of the land – but the villagers had told the tale because they were hoping it was so, and it was not long before many Aurovilians were fully engaged in tree planting, water conservation and organic farming. The coming of Auroville sparked a variety of hopes for a better life in the minds of the villagers. Some sold their land to Auroville and bought better land elsewhere; some came to work in Auroville, mostly starting as manual labourers and household helpers; some did business

with Auroville, providing building materials and work teams; many learned to speak English. The people who came to work for Auroville found they were treated not just as labourers but as "real people", and the bright ones were recognised and promoted to responsible positions. Many children saw the friendly foreigners as a source of nourishment for their hunger for education, and Aurovilians responded with schools for the children. Of course, many villagers were too busy to take much notice of Auroville – either with their own village politics, or with the pressing need to provide food for themselves and family. And a few saw Auroville just as a target for theft.

1973 - The first time happy women and children from Kuilapalayam are collecting water from a Fraternity well source. Before they had to collect the water in clay pots from down near the beach.

Cars visiting Auroville from Pondicherry could easily run into difficult situations.

The roads in Auroville were sandy and sometimes muddy, and when you took a wrong turn you could land up in a virtual quagmire. But friendly helpful local villagers were there to move the car with casuarina poles and manpower back onto the road.

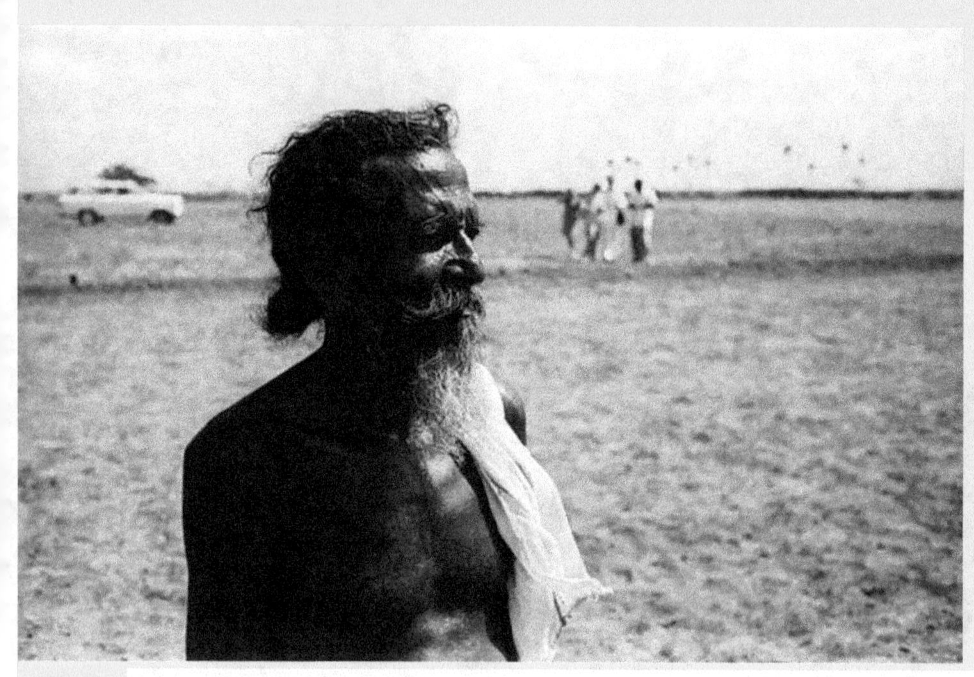

Mutual help

At the same time, villagers were teaching the Aurovilians about the local agricultural practices, language and culture. The villagers' simple worship of local idols didn't fully transmit the rich Dravidian tradition of great yogis called "Siddhas", who had achieved great psychic powers through their tapasya, but their bright smiles, endurance and helpfulness even in the midst of such hardship testified to a deeply instilled spirituality. In those days Auroville provided a mid-day lunch to most of its employees, but also there were instances when workers not only didn't get paid, but brought food to their temporarily-out-of-funds Aurovilian employers!

Charlie and others remember...

"For me early Auroville was fantastic, simple – simple for the people. Later in the day, I remember going up that hill, Pitchandikulam, Certitude. There was nothing, nothing! I didn't know about Forecomers yet. Auroson's Home was just a tile roof house. Frederick and Shyama were there. The Nursery was there with some pots, but no-one lived there. There was the urn. A guy stayed near by, Guido, I think, maybe with Diana. There was one hut there. The excavation (for Matrimandir foundations) had not started.

"I remember going up that hill, and half way up stopping in the blazing sun of mid summer. It was there that somehow I decided: this Auroville is fantastic. I had read the Auroville Charter, and it was a great Charter.

Field workers from the surrounding villages coming together, a white cloth turban (thalapa) their only protection again the blazing sun.

I looked around, there was nothing, and I thought: this is a fantastic place, like the new world. It didn't deter me at all that there was nothing out here. As a matter of fact, it was even better, that there was nothing! I thought, this is a great place; I have got to be here.

"I started to work at the Nursery carrying water for the plants. Narad was there. Basically it was only pots. When they started the Matrimandir excavation, I started working there. I used to cycle out to Auroville every day."

Turning Points

"We were living in the middle of the fields, sleeping in the fields, there were no trees. The water used to come by kattavandi. We would wait and see in the distance the kattavandi coming with the water. It was timeless. There was no electricity, no village music. It was still the ragi culture here; there was this amazing cycle of timelessness. I don't know if you have ever ploughed a field with bullocks, it is an amazing feeling. Watching them is different, but if you do it yourself, you feel an amazing security. This is a wonderful thing, ploughing the field. It is so ancient. India was really incredible. Now with TV and everything it is totally ruined. It is not the same thing."

Roy

"When you came from the Pondicherry-Madras coast road to Kuilapalayam village, the right side of the road was completely undeveloped. There were just the tamarind

1972 – Kuilapalayam kids ▼
1971 – Banyan Tree

1978 – Green Belt road between Two Banyans and Utility

trees to the north of the village, and then further on came the kambu and peanut fields. The landscape was flat as far as the horizon, with only a few palmyra trees to be seen. You could see to the east the ocean, and in the other direction – somewhere in the distance – the Matrimandir under construction. We had sandstorms and beautiful sunsets. There were two roads connecting Aspiration and Kuilapalayam with Pondicherry. One was via Bommayapalayam and the other was a sand road following a canyon towards the beach road. We could make it on the bicycle, mostly pushing it through the sand patches, or bullock carts could use this sandy short-cut to travel to Pondicherry. There was also no well in the village, and water had to be carried in water

kujas from down near the beach. When Fraternity with its first workshops was started, the area was fenced with a small wall, and cacti were planted on top to keep the goats and cows out. When the first trees were planted, there was no planned layout; they were just planted for shade. Later, together with the workshops, a water tank was constructed, connected initially to a new small well, then a deeper well, from which pipes were connected and taps installed to give the villagers a better water supply."

Franz

"My best friends were in Fertile. I went there and helped plant part of the Fertile forest. Then I was looking at this land here [Fertile Windmill] where there was

1976 – Fraternity early plantation and orchard. A wall of cactus plants forms the borders of the community land.

nothing, and I said: I want to put a forest here. I put up a little hut, it cost me two hundred rupees at the time. There was nothing else. From here you could see the Banyan. Everybody thought I was mad. There was no road, no water, no fence, no nothing. I had a few books, a mat, a kerosene lamp (which they stole the first day), and I lived there for a year. The motorbike track became the road, we put up a windmill and we started planting trees. That was the beginning."

Vijay

"In those days, Auroville was an immense barren plateau swept by dust winds in summer and devastated during the monsoons by heavy downpours which washed away the top-soil and the red soil, flushing it into the nearby ocean via heavily eroded canyons. One could see very few trees except around villages. There were three hamlets with some huts built with mud and covered with palm leaves. In 1972, the largest community in Auroville was called Aspiration; it was the first halting place on this plateau, which you reached through a path meandering along a canyon. There, at the edge of Kuilapalayam village, there were huts of a different kind, covered with straw. It was in this place that most of the "Aurovilians", as the Mother called them, lived."

Paul Vincent

Tree planting: local workers are using mumptis for digging holes in the sandy red soil.

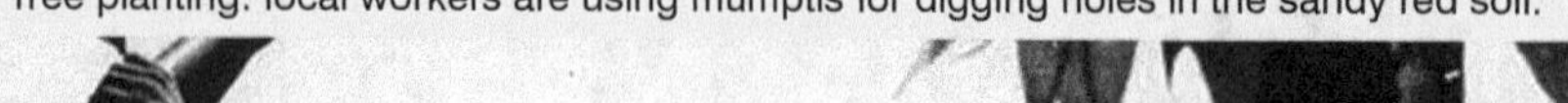

New ways

It was clear, however, that the answer to the people's poverty didn't lie in the past, but in the NOW, inspired by a new hope for the future. Auroville, focused on the coming of a new era of life on earth, promised this new future for all, and the early Aurovilians together with the eager-for-a-job villagers began to work together to redeem the land. Ecologically, the land was restored with earth bunds, tree planting, protection and farming.

Economically, the people were earning enough to improve their diet, fix their leaking roofs, and send their children to school. A Health Centre was set up to deal with the many illnesses among the population. Also, as Auroville began to grow, villagers were engaged and trained in construction trades, and managerial skills were built up.

A variety of small handicraft units devoted to skills like incense making, needlework and leatherwork sprang up, often in Aurovilians' houses, and a large number of local women learned such skills; increased their family income; and confronted a new style of living.

At the same time, other Aurovilians were responding to the cry of the children for education. Schools for village children were set up, and some children were adopted into the Auroville community, singly or in small residential educational experiments. Now, some 45 years later, many of these children are pillars of the Auroville community. And many environmental working groups, undertakings, village oriented activities and development projects are ongoing.

Aurovilians and local workers planting and watering young trees.

Greening the canyon

The check-dams change nature considerably. There is a definite greening going on in the canyons where, a few years back, check-dams were built. Trees, bushes, creepers and other plants have spontaneously emerged. This would only happen if it would rain a few dozen centimetres daily for at least a week. Within a few years they will provide an impenetrable barrier, provided that the villagers don't cut too many trees for firewood. The explosive greening, however, is not to everyone's liking. Aurovilians who love to go on nature discovery tours complain that canyon walks have become all but impossible. The flora ensures that rainwater seeps more quickly into the ground and holds the red earth and the topsoil, which otherwise would flow into the Bay of Bengal.

The early canyon at Utility with its bizarre-looking "moon" landscape.

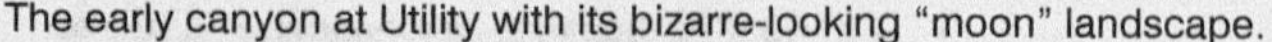

The earth remains wet for a longer period, and that in turn stimulates more plants to grow. And without any need for human intervention, the canyon's biotopes recover.

The beginning of this process can be witnessed in the Utility canyon. The white sand is being covered by red earth, the first grasses come up and small plants mature. Its flowers attract insects and large, colourful butterflies, which in turn provide food for small mammals, reptiles and birds. There are wagtails, brahminy kites, shikras (a small hawk), the hawk cuckoo – also known as the brain-fever bird, green bee-eaters, metallic-blue kingfishers, red-whiskered bulbuls, hoopoes and, last but not least, the Indian great horned owl. This is an impressive bird, who loves the canyon, sitting on a perch watching for prey.

A check-dam in the Utility canyon now holds the monsoon rains, inviting youth from the village to take a dip.

Auroville

Red earth
The folded leaf
A trembling dream

The well drilled
Granite fences
Growth incorporated

Accelerated bruises
A rattling cart
Matter transformed

Without my cloak
I come
The youthful fool

Unending education
Willing servant
No easy task.

Vitthal

An area of red canyon in Auroville shaped by heavy monsoon rains.

From Aspiration to the beach road

Just about everyone rode them, the heavy Atlas and Hero bicycles with which we negotiated the winding cart path from Aspiration to the beach road. That's how you traveled to Pondy. The best time was early in the morning. You stood on the edge of the Auroville plateau to watch the fireball rise out of the ocean, then pushed off into the corridor that wound between the peanut fields, barren except when the plants appeared around September.

Going down was relatively easy: just keep an eye on the sand traps which sucked your wheels in and brought the cycle to a halt; glide on the inclines. The weight of your Atlas would pull you through. At times, in some of the more eroded sections, it almost seemed that the fields were above you. And watch out for ascending bullock carts. One time, seduced by the new green of the peanuts, I pulled to the side for one of them to pass me. But the driver was dozing, and suddenly I felt the wooden wheels crunching over my wheels, bending them into a curled up dosai. Even an Atlas isn't that strong. I walked it down the road, where there were bicycle repair huts every kilometre, and the guy straightened them enough for me to continue.

The tar road was a relief after that, with patches of shade. Local buses lumbered past and a few Ambassador cars, but the traffic was minimal. Muthialpet was the same bottleneck it is today, but there was a side street running

1968-75 - Bicycles were the only form of transport to reach Pondicherry, via a sandy road leading down from Aspiration community to the beach road.

parallel to the main road, lined with traditional Tamilian houses, that brought you out at the Handmade Paper Factory.

Pumping those cycles back up the sand path in the sun would mean a sweat-drenched struggle and some trudging through the sand dune sections. A heavy load on your back carrier meant more walking. When you reached the top and looked back, however, there was a sense of accomplishment at having ascended a minor peak.

The best time to return was at night when there was a moon. Once a week we rode to Pondy for a meditation with Yvonne Artaud in her flat near the ocean, and then returned around nine. The clamour of the Muthialpet bazaar was winding down, and once clear of it the road cleared also. Some of us may have had lights, and the others followed them. Moonlight was the best time to travel. Once we made the Auroville turn, marked by a single abandoned building, road noise receded and we climbed steadily. The air was cool and the moonlight made us think, perhaps, that the sand was a pale snow tugging at our wheels. Then we reached the little Hobbit huts of Aspiration and the scattered kerosene lamps of Kuilapalayam.

Slide the lock closed on the faithful Atlas. The lights of Pondy in the distance were so faint that you might distinguish the Southern Cross constellation on the horizon. Tired and time for bed.

Gordon

1980 - A sandy stretch of road from the Green Belt to Utility, going on down to Bommayapalayam.

First permanent house construction
and landscaping in Auromodele, 1979.
Auromodele was designed as a
trial site for future residential houses
in Auroville.

The first houses in Auromodele look
very futuristic, the round shaped
red walls are formed like huge sculptures
with the white curved roofs
confronting the blue sky and sun.

Bamboo plants and 'work' trees,
the first green colours in the otherwise
red barren landscape.
From an inner courtyard a wooden
staircase leads to the first floor.

A lotus pond surrounds
the red building, with
granite stones forming the bridge
that leads into the building.

Poppo had his first taste in landscaping, transforming the space around the huge banyan tree into a garden (10,000 sq m) in Promesse, the first community of Auroville. He used Japanese elements in his design and layout of this garden. He experimented, creating landscapes with local materials, slabs of granite and stone, setting each piece with his own hands.

"To work with rocks is contagious:" Spending hours tending to the garden, he realised how important it was to work with hardy indigenous plants to save time and water. Many of the lessons he learned there bore fruit over the years as he refined his natural tendency towards creating landscapes that look as if they have always existed, and don't cry out for attention.

"Landscape was never in my mind consciously except through my love for nature... Today it has evolved into an inseparable part between the inside and outside. For practical reasons we need this distinction to divide and to demarcate, but for me, ideally, design doesn't consider this distinction. There is no inside and outside. I see all as a flow, all evolves together, jumping over seeming boundaries to include all, permanently changing surfaces into others ... leaning onto each other, mingling with each other, creating vistas, surprises [. . .] Nature is not ornamental."

Poppo Pingel

Inscription
Pipal Garden, Promesse, 1977

The first Auroville Japanese Tea House was built in Promesse.

A rocky promontory leads to stepping stones across a pool.

A brick-paved path passes a banyan, with granite benches forming a defining perimeter.

1974, workshops and kindergarden are constructed by Poppo in Fraternity. Landscaping with granite stones and granite pilliars. Only cactus plants and Palmyra trees can remain stable and grow on the red dry land.

Fraternity workshops were designed to hold the newly established weaving unit and the kindergarten for the village children whose mothers were employed in Auroville.

Poppo Pingel

Kambu fields flooded by monsoon rains.

An early, dome-shaped house made using local materials. ▶

Bullock cart on the sandy road from Aspiration to Pondicherry, 1974

Auroville's afforestation

Auroville's afforestation campaign began in the early 1970s. The first tree nurseries were started in Success and Kottakarai and, with the help of grants from the Point Foundation, the Tamil Fund and friends abroad, large-scale tree planting began. In the next ten years, as part of a massive soil and water conservation programme, over a million trees – timber, ornamental, fencing, fruit and fodder trees, nut trees, etc – were planted in Auroville. Some were exotic, like the Australian "Work Tree" (Acacia auriculiformis), which has adapted so well that it is now crowding out other species. As the trees grew and micro-climates formed, many species of birds, animals and other wildlife returned, further accelerating the dissemination of seeds and enriching the environment.

Outreach

In 1982, impressed by the success of the afforestation project, the Department of Environment, Government of India, offered Auroville 11 lakhs of rupees (then around US $100,000) over five years to plant trees and scientifically monitor the results so that the most appropriate techniques and species for our situation – which is the situation of many other parts of India – could be identified. It was the beginning of a new orientation for greenworkers in Auroville, for now it became evident that Auroville had something precious to offer beyond its own boundaries.

Earlier view of the eucalyptus grove, coming from Certitude community, as it was before cyclone Thane.

In the past few years, this "outreach" has intensified. Further grants from the Government and from organisations abroad have enabled Auroville to run courses in afforestation for villagers, social workers, tribals, academics and administrators. The results are not always encouraging – the follow-up work of the trainees is sometimes poor or non-existent – but the success stories are dramatic. In 1987, for example, a Swiss Aid-sponsored project brought a group of tribals from the central Indian states to Auroville. Coming from areas which were almost totally deforested, they were inspired by what they saw here and returned determined to change their environment. That year, in Rajasthan, they planted 328,000 trees; the next year they planted 1,600,000 – and with an 85% survival rate! Other educational initiatives taking place in Auroville include courses run by a Dutch organization called Agriculture, Man and Ecology (AME), drawing participants from all over south-east Asia, and a project to design and produce environmental education materials for schools.

At the same time, Aurovilian greenworkers have been increasingly going out into India to share their experience and help initiate new afforestation schemes. These have included projects with Tibetan refugees in Karnataka, with Irula tribesmen near Chinglepet in Tamil Nadu, and a massive project funded by the National Wastelands Commission in the Palani Hills to re-afforest large areas near Dindigul and Kodaikanal.

July 1989

A sandy path leads through the Auroville forest.

Matrimandir

O soul of our City
Centre of Clarity
House of our Peace
    Heart of the Matter
    Eye of the Storm
    Life of the Party
Rising Sign
Light in our Eyes
Gilded Cage

Mystery of Matter
Concrete Embodiment
    Ball of the Game
Shell of our Prayer
Shrine to our Mother
Ten thousand Songs
    Sigh of the Earth
    Sweet Honeycomb
    Mirror of the Sun

Radiance of our Joy
Convergence of our Trials and Errors
Oneness
    O Soul of our City
    Crystallise
    Infinite Longing

1975 - Sunrise behind the Matrimandir, still under construction.

Quo Vadis

Yenge po?
Where to?
E dove va?
'I go to the market
To buy a fat pig...'
C'est la vie hélas!
Mondo Cane!

Nan Yar?
Qui suis-je?
Who?
'I am the pussy in the well.
Who put her in?'
C'est moi, hélas!
Mondo Cane!

Yenge po?
Whereto?
Quo vadis?
'Little Jack Horner
Sits in his Corner...'
At New Creation!
Mondo Cane!

View from the eucalyptus grove

Dark Clouds

We are the thunderstorms and sided rains,
The scattered zig-zag lines, the burst and blast,
The floods, the ravages and deaths.
We are Asuras of the night,
The traitors.

We say: it doesn't have to be today!
In ancient swamps black crocodiles
Feed on bright dragonflies...
Before starlight were we poured out
Like water.

We ride our shadow on charred lands.
We shape our images in pride and reddish clay,
A sad king or a sobbing clown...
Does not the nectar of chanting flow in our veins?
Darkest Bhajan.

Heavy monsoon clouds over the water catchment tank at Irumbai.

Sundance

We are the people of the sun;
The dancers and the dance,
Deep music in our bone.
Now we have begun:
Our tools are gleaming in array.
Today the war is won.
Unseen our work is done:
Together Sound and Silence
Dancing in the Sun...

Greeting!

I wish you the Roar of the Lion,
And the Silence of a Fish,
The Patience of a Tree,
The Freedom of the Sky,
And the Love of the Great Heart
In which we have our Being!

All 5 poems on pp. 64-67 by Vitthal

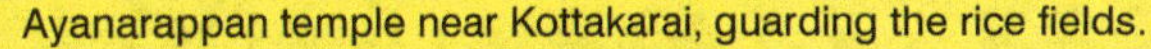

Ayanarappan temple near Kottakarai, guarding the rice fields.

Gardens in Auroville

One of the most beautiful ornamental gardens in Auroville is situated at Gaia's Garden Guest House on the road from Kuilapalayam to Bommayapalayam. Its abundance of plants of diverse colour and texture is breathtaking. They have been planted with an artist's eye. In between you spot statues of a reclining Ganesh or a dancing Shiva.

"I spend two hours each morning working in the garden," says Dutch Aurovilian Kireet. "It is my great joy, and the guests, too, enjoy the garden." But there were many trials and errors before it reached its present form. "This land was a cashew tope before I came and the soil was acidic and poor. It took years to get restored."

Kireet began repeating the patterns of the gardens he had built in The Netherlands. "But I soon realized that this was not going to work here. I had to learn about tropical

Gaia's Garden

plants." So for two years, he worked at the Matrimandir Nursery and at Shakti Nursery studying cultivars and indigenous plants. "I would join the seed expeditions to the scrub jungles or the temple groves to collect seeds. During these trips, I would collect plants and started experimenting with them, putting them at different places in Gaia's Garden, seeing where they survived. Many died, but in the process I made discoveries and learned a lot.

"A garden is never finished; it is always a work in progress. Now I am in the phase where I want to make it more detailed and create hidden corners or a 'secret garden' as it were. So there is the element of surprise, of the unexpected, and each time you visit it another discovery awaits you. A garden takes time, but that doesn't matter, because at every stage it has this rewarding beauty."

A stone Ganesh rests in front of a rich green plant background

In his heart Kireet is a gardener

Gardening is an important part of Kireet's daily life. In nature and in a beautiful garden he feels close to Gaia, Mother Earth, and to the Divine. To work with his hands in the earth is essential for his well-being.

A garden is not a forest, although an untouched natural forest has its own beauty, which cannot be equaled by human effort. Unfortunately these forests are rare nowadays. Tropical gardening is a constant challenge.

Gardening is very personal, and there are as many gardens as gardeners. Of course to create something special there are garden principles to be considered.

First there are the paths and open spaces. The details can be filled in later, when the garden reaches more maturity. Much must also be left to the inspiration of the gardener. It is the eye only that will finally say if the garden is beautiful.

Planting the garden is just the beginning, because it will take years to grow and reach a certain maturity. Gardening is mostly maintenance, preferably daily, and with it growth; it changes all the time. A large garden needs trees. Without trees any garden becomes dull after a while. In our tropical climate shade is essential. If gardens cannot give shade and coolness, then who likes to be in them?

Then harmony is an important aspect. A successful garden is a garden which looks as though it fell

Ikekomi-gata stone lantern.

A lush garden with a few
Japanese *Ikekomi-gata* stone lanterns,
and also modern elements
like swimming stone rings
carrying white quartz stones.

into place by itself. A uniform ground cover, like grass, pebbles or even sand, will bind the different parts and features together. The ground covers should make a definite and coherent pattern throughout the garden. The textures and the patterns of the different ground covers set the tone of the whole design of the garden. The challenge of a harmonious and interesting garden is finding the exact balance between unity and variety. The important thing to remember is to keep clean lines along the paths and avoid too many details. For that reason it is better to form groups of plants or shrubs together, which are linked with the other plants. In large gardens careful massing of similar and contrasting colours and tones can give spectacular effects. Large groups of a single colour are more effective than mixtures. Mixing colours is a delicate matter. It is better to have one dominant colour. A garden

A path with granite slabs, and a *Ikekomi-gata* stone lantern with white quartz stones around it.

must give an impression of space. It can be helpful to keep the middle open and the plants on the sides.

The lower branches of big trees need to be pruned. This increases the sense of space, when you can look through certain corridors. This is a more Western approach. The Japanese way of creating a feeling of space is more sophisticated, and requires greater sensitivity and a very true eye. We learn from the Japanese to eliminate from the garden everything which is not essential for its beauty. This is, as a gardener, sometimes difficult, and he has to look at the garden with a different mood. Each plant has to be in its right place. To look at the garden details from different angles is also helpful. But at the same time Kireet likes gardens which look natural and smell wild. He likes to see what surprises nature has, which seeds come spontaneously, and how to let them

An arched metal gate with creepers leads to the inner part of the garden.

fit in. He likes daring natural combinations, though that can be very risky.

A garden changes all the time. Constant adjustments and changes are needed to keep pace with its changing character. Always trying to improve in order to create something beautiful. Garden principles are not enough, when one tries to capture something beyond.

The greatest mark of success is when a garden achieves a look of timelessness, a look of eternity. It looks as though it has existed since the beginning of time, and will continue to exist until the end.

Light is an overwhelmingly important factor. A garden can look completely different at different times of the day. The quality of the shade given by a tree is then an important factor.

Trees with small leaves give a light shade, but trees like the Service tree, with its fairly dense foliage, give a cool shade, even at midday.

The shade of a Realisation tree is not cool enough for that, but a single Realisation on a lawn casts a beautiful pattern of light and shade on the grass. A garden must have a shifting harmony of different qualities of light and shade. It may express then a mystical atmosphere, and gardening may become a spiritual exercise. Maybe that's why one can be full of joy in a garden.

Gerard Jak (Kireet)

Calabash-tree, *Crescentua cujete*

Granite benches circle a banyan tree.

View from Gaia's Garden guest house terrace onto the garden below.

Residence with garden showing Japanese influence.

Modern contemporary architecture
amid a garden with both
Indian and Japanese elements.

Containers chipped
out of single rocks.

Tachi-gata stone lanterns
balanced by plants, bushes
and granite slabs.

House in Japanese style with garden

A wooden house in Japanese style
surrounded by
a beautiful garden.

Architecture, rocks and plants
form a composition with a Zen touch.

A beautiful lush tropical garden
with carefully trimmed plants and bushes beside the path.

Softer, mainly green landscapes.

Pitanga

The small concrete path
leading to Pitanga Hall
passes a Chinese Banyan
or Indian Laurel tree,
Ficus microcarp.
with many air roots falling
from its branches.

The inner courtyard
of Pitanga
has a small garden
with a water pool
and fountain.

Pitanga entrance and garden

A boulder wall and plant nursery

A raised pathway passes bamboo greenery outside a Japanese-style
guest house with surrounding garden

Sharnga Tai Chi Hall is constructed in teak wood, in South Indian style. The hall on the roof of the residential house is surrounded by freely shaped and grown gardens.

Garden space and lotus ponds
surrounding houses.

◄ A tiled pathway; brick lines used
to define differing garden areas;
and a granite slab pathway.

◄ A path paved with granite stabs
leads to a house,
passing several work trees.

Strong use of granite slabs in a modern garden landscape.

Walls made out of bricks and granite boulders.

A cactus garden contrasts with a smooth domed residence.

A joined building entrance, using a mixture ▶
of materials and colour tones to good effect.

Path paved with bricks and a precast garden lamp in front.

Guest houses with balcony and view to the beach.

The Quiet Healing Centre is now heavily affected by beach erosion, with more than a hundred metres of beach lost. The photos show the land and garden before this happened.

A path leads to the Quiet Healing Centre reception office.

Leaves of lotus plants reflecting the sun.

Quiet Healing Centre – an earlier view down to the beach.

The plant to which Mother gave the name Concentration.

The white dome-shaped roof of the Quiet Healing Centre.

Front view of the Quiet Healing Centre.

Reception building, looking out over the Bay of Bengal

Zen gardens

Lastly, there are the Japanese-inspired Zen gardens. One, situated at Afsanah Guest House, is placed behind the dining hall. The garden, dominated by rock and sand, is surrounded by large trees which, in their own way, echo its innate tranquillity. "Our guests love this garden," says Afsaneh, the guest house manager.

It was designed by Poppo, who lives next door and has his own Zen garden at the back of his house, almost three times the size of the one at the guest house. Bamboo groves, mossy pathways, bonsai trees and objets trouvé surround this garden, creating an atmosphere inviting contemplation. Poppo, who has never been to Japan, but says "Japan comes here," emphasises the enormous amount of time and dedication it takes to develop and maintain a beautiful garden. This is one of five Japanese-style gardens he has created during his years in Auroville.

Contrast between cut granite pillars and soft rounded boulders.

Afsanah Guest House dining hall with surrounding garden.

"It started out as an instinct to create a garden, a small one, simply in front of our house in Promesse," he says.

"But it grew bigger and bigger, and automatically led to a lifelong trip of landscaping."

"Start small," he advises. "A garden is never 'ready made'. Learn to really look at the plants. See where they are happy to grow. Then the potential is enormous – it grows and you grow at the same time."

Afsanah Guest House: another view of the pond and garden outside the dining hall.

"The mind imposes itself on landscape (nature). It shows either in geometrical patterns, military alignments, strangled amputation or other unnatural formations like modern neo-rococo style as doubtfully mind-sense-pleasing "Kitsch", contrary to the nature of nature's play with itself."

Poppo, 25.7.2012

"A harmonic landscape is a conscious play between man and receptive nature."

Poppo, 31.07.2012

Behind the main entrance building is a Zen rock garden, with rocks transported from the Mailam area.

"Nature's nature is to adapt itself to other natures, expand, grow into, lean on each other, or to die. Humans have the tendency to decorate nature, bring in mental ideas, formulate to make it 'look good' so that they feel pleased…"

Poppo, 27.10.2012

The paths between the guest bungalows are artistically laid out with granite slabs; some stretches are formed with pieces of tiles and other ceramic elements.

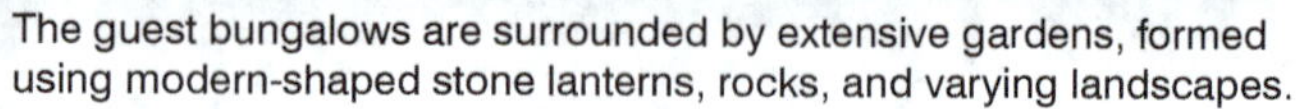

The guest bungalows are surrounded by extensive gardens, formed using modern-shaped stone lanterns, rocks, and varying landscapes.

"If we (humans) don't respect nature, nature will not in the long run "respect" us. Nature doesn't think! The opening of a flower blossom or the cataclysm of volcanoes is "unthought". Nature takes us (humans) by surprise, that is its beauty. We have to collaborate with Nature and not impose."
15.08.2012

"A garden is a conscious (or unconscious) interference in nature of any kind. Nature has no need of a garden as such. It creates spontaneously gardens of infinite character according to its own laws and conditions without any mental explanation of our human superiority."
Poppo, 15.8.2012

Residential house with Zen garden. The laterite stones in this garden came from Edayanchavadi village.

"Architecture is all-embracing when it concerns the human being. Nature is integral, intertwining and complex."

19 April 2009

House entrance (below) with a megalitic urn.

A drainage channel with rocks and granite slabs for running off rainwater

Grinding stones, granite pillars,
and amid bamboo poles
a bronze statue of a meditating Buddha.
In front the round basin, a typical *tsukubai*,
contrasts with the rough stones

"Everything is landscape, wherever creation happens is landscape, here, be it cloudscape, the free skyscape, or forest, meadow, desert, moonscape."

26.7.2012

Grinding stones used as stepping stones, statues from South India, and a collection of Bonzai trees.

A statue of a meditating Buddha, and behind a target for archery.

The Botanical Gardens

The Auroville Botanical Gardens was started in August 2000 on 50 acres of old cashew land rescued from the threat of real estate development. The Gardens have seen a dramatic growth since then. More than 260 tree species have been planted in the 30-acre arboretum; 5,500 specimens have been planted in the 10-acre conservation forest; and a TDEF plant nursery has been created, capable of producing 50,000 seedlings per year to promote widespread re-introduction of the indigenous flora of the region.

The Auroville Botanical Gardens has as its special mission the conservation and preservation of the Tropical Dry Evergreen Forest (TDEF). This forest-type, unique to India's south-eastern sea-board and once extending from Vishakhapatnam in the north to Ramanathapuram in the south, has all but disappeared except for a few pockets around sacred groves. It is now reduced to less than 1% of its original area.

Since Auroville's inception, teams of green workers involved in the reforestation work of Auroville have been making trips to sacred groves to collect seeds of the native TDEF species. But a survey done by the Botanical Gardens two years ago has shown that sacred groves are rapidly shrinking in size. Encroachment is rampant. Fortunately with Auroville now having all the native TDEF species, seed collection happens within Auroville itself.

Another prime focus of the Gardens is education. A constant flow of groups from the 40-odd schools in the area, including Auroville schools, plus some from further afield, come for study visits. At the Environmental Education Centre they learn about the importance of conserving the TDEF, and then visit the arboretum to see the actual trees. They can also visit other specialist gardens such as the cactus and orchid gardens, and learn about how plants and insects evolve together. The overall aim is to help the younger generation better appreciate and understand nature, thereby instilling in them a desire to protect and preserve it.

The Botanical Garden has 50 acres of land and was started in the year 2000.

The Shakti Nursery in Auroville is primarily engaged in the conservation and propagation of the Tropical Dry Evergeen Forest (TDEF). The nursery is part of a wider project that aims at re-creating the indigenous forest in the Green Belt area of Auroville.

Shakti nursery is a park and garden area next to Aspiration community. Many new plants start growing here, and are then later planted elsewhere in Auroville or other places in Tamil Nadu.

Tending to young growing plants in Shakti Nursery

Matrimandir Nursery

Matrimandir Nursery was the first garden area in Auroville.
It has many mature trees,
and today provides plants for the Matrimandir Gardens.

Mahalakshmi Park

Mahalakshmi Park is an area separating the Matrimandir Gardens and the Residential Zone, stretching from the Solar Kitchen to Gaia.

New trees and newly placed rocks form this new park area.

Rocks from Mailam area are widely used to strengthen and give character to the landscape (no such rocks exist naturally in the Auroville area).

Matrimandir Park and Gardens

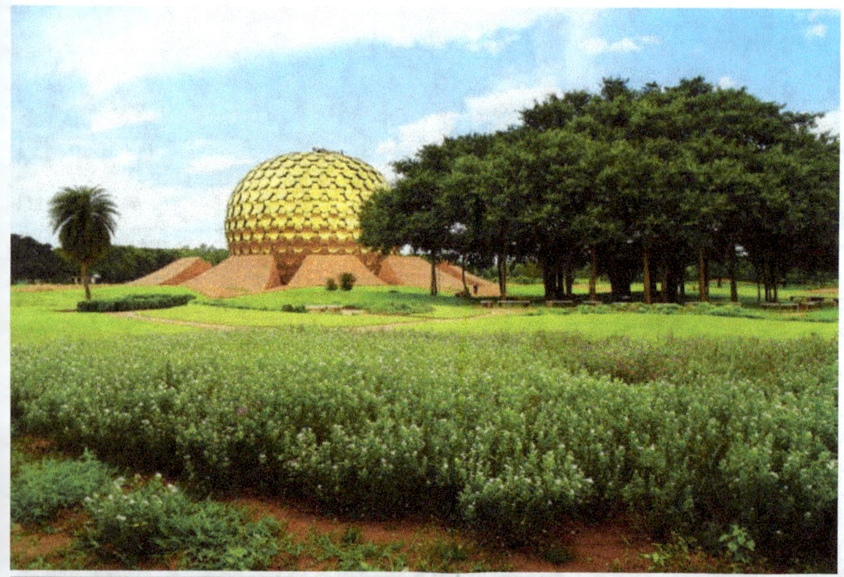

The gardens and the landscape
of the Matrimandir Gardens are still being developed.

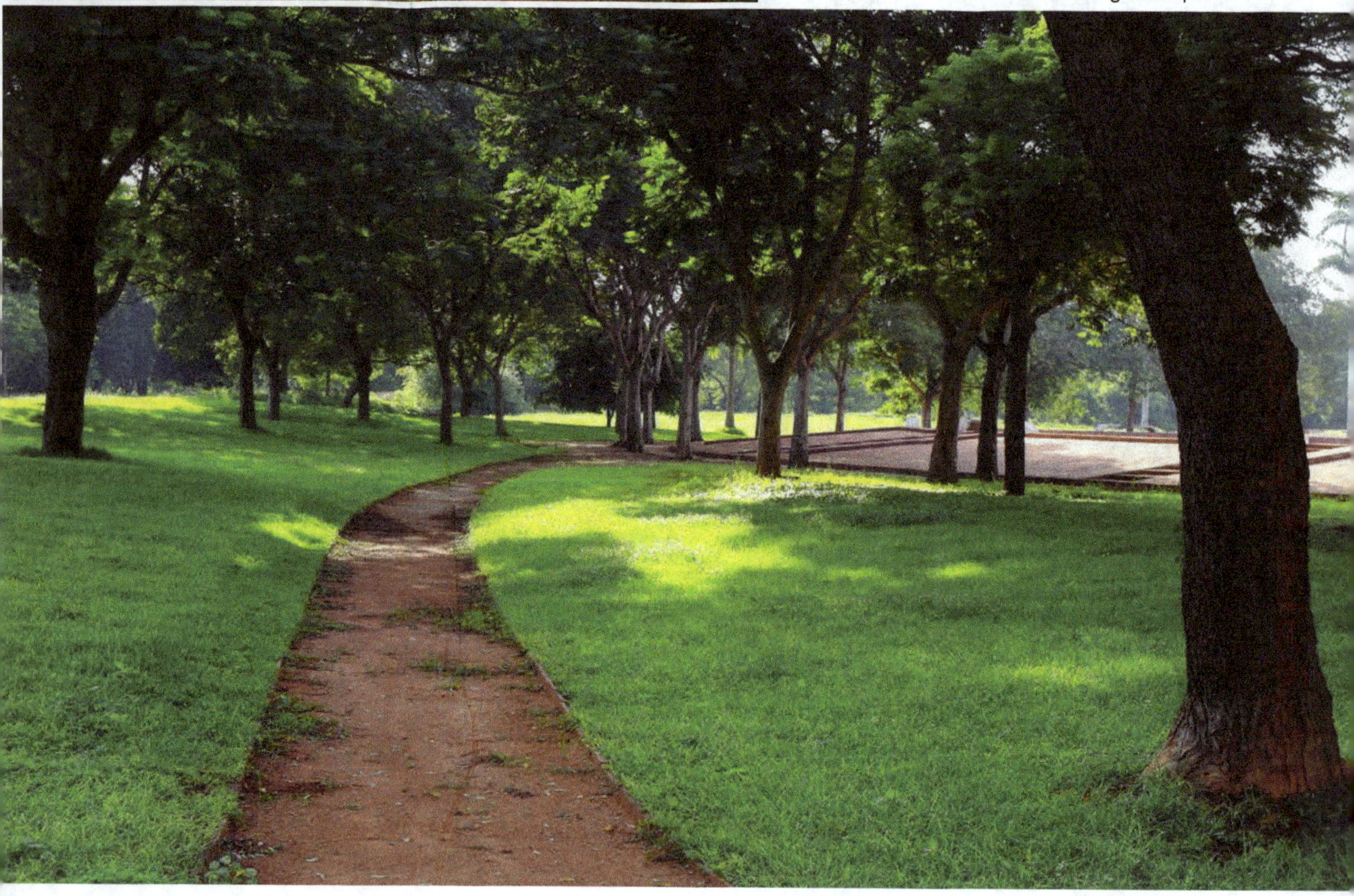

A study for the twelve Matrimandir gardens, surrounded by a lake,
by Paolo Tommasi, 15 August 2002.

My plan is very simple

It will be up there, off the Madras road, on top of the hill. (Mother takes a piece of paper and starts drawing) Here we have (naturally in Nature it's not like this: we'll have to adapt – it's like this up there, in the ideal), here, a central point. This central point is a park I had seen when I was a little girl (perhaps the most beautiful thing in the world with regard to physical, material Nature), a park with water and trees like all parks, and flowers, but not too many (flowers in the form of creepers), palm trees and ferns (all species of palm trees), water (if possible, running water) and, if possible, a small waterfall. From a practical point of view, it would be very good: at the edge, outside the park, we could build reservoirs that would provide water to the residents.

The Mother

Bird's eye view of the Matrimandir Peace area facing east.

These gardens... we had thought of twelve gardens

So [the architect] had arranged a whole system of bridges to link it to the other bank. And the other bank would be composed entirely of gardens all around. These gardens... we had thought of twelve gardens (of dividing the distance by twelve), of making twelve gardens, each concentrated on one thing: a particular state of consciousness and the flowers that represent it. And then the twelfth garden would be in the water, around (not around, but beside) the *Mandir* and with the Banyan tree which is there. That's what is at the centre of the city. And there, there would be a repetition of the twelve gardens which surround it with the flowers similarly arranged…

The Mother

An early model proposed by Paolo Tommasi for the future Matrimandir Gardens and lake.

The flowers of Auroville

Mother chose a variety of hibiscus which she had already called "Beauty of Supramental Love" as the symbol of Auroville and she made the following comment: "It urges us to live at its height".

The first hibiscus chosen by Mother as the emblem of Auroville was "Godhead", of which she wrote: "Pure and perfect, projects its force into the world". It is a large single flower of the Hawaiian variety, cream in colour with a rose centre and crinkled petals.

Godhead
Pure and perfect, puts forth its force in the world.

Beauty of Supramental Love
It invites us to learn to live at its height.

Beauty of the new creation (Beauty of Auroville)
The new creation strives to better manifest the Divine.

Power of spiritual beauty (Spiritual beauty of Auroville)
Spiritual beauty has a contagious power.

But later on, seeing another variety, "Beauty of Supramental Love", she gave it first place, because this flower is almost the same colour as the earth of Auroville. "Godhead" remains nevertheless one of the flowers of Auroville.

Mother also chose special hibiscus flowers for most of the gardens which will surround the Matrimandir. Later on she attributed special qualities of Auroville to several varieties of hibiscus.

Sri Aurobindo's Action

Charm of the new creation (Charm of Auroville)
The new creation is attractive to all those who want to progress.

Concentration of the new creation (Concentration of Auroville)
Concentration on a precise goal is helpful to development.

Sweetness of power surrendered to the Divine (Sweetness of Auroville)
Sweetness itself becomes powerful when it is at the service of the Divine.

Power of effort (Effort of Auroville)
Effort well-directed overcomes all obstacles.

New Creation

The only creation for which there is any place here is the Supramental, the bringing of the divine Truth down on the earth, not only into the mind and vital but into the body and into Matter... We are here to do what the Divine wills and to create a world in which the Divine Will can manifest its truth no longer deformed by human ignorance or perverted and mistranslated by vital desire. The work which the sadhak of the Supramental Yoga has to do is not his own work, for which he can lay down his own conditions, but the work of the Divine, which he has to do

Blossoming of the new creation (Blossoming of Auroville)
The more we concentrate on the goal,
the more it blossoms forth and becomes precise.

Firmness of the new creation (Firmness of Auroville)
The new creation wants to be steadfast in its manifestation.

Manifold power of the new creation (Manifold power of Auroville)
The new creation will be rich in possibilities.

Ideal of the new creation (Ideal of Auroville)
The ideal should be progressive so that it can be realised in the future.

according to the conditions laid down by the Divine. Our yoga is not for our own sake but for the sake of the Divine.

The Supramental creation, since it has to be a creation upon earth, must be not only an inner change but a physical and external manifestation also... It is the actual descent of the Supramental Divine into Matter and the working of the Divine Presence and Power there that can alone make the physical and external change possible.

Sri Aurobindo

Progress of the new creation (Progress of Auroville)
Each must find the activity favourable to his progress.

Realisation of the new creation (Realisation of Auroville)
It is for this that we must prepare.

Power of success (Success of Auroville)
The power of those who know how to continue their effort.

Usefulness of the new creation (Usefulness of Auroville)
A creation which aims at teaching men to surpass themselves.

The Mother on Matrimandir Gardens

So in that park I had seen the "Pavilion of Love" (but I don't like to use the word because men have turned it into something ludicrous); I am referring to the principle of divine Love. But it has been changed; it will be "the Pavilion of the Mother"; but not this *(Mother points to Herself)*: the Mother, the true Mother, the principle of the Mother. This is the centre.

All around, there is a circular road that separates the park from the rest of the city.

The park, too, I saw – those are old visions I had repeatedly.

Ah! Now the Mother's Pavilion – it will be surrounded by a lake, tall trees, various kinds of flowers – I especially want the creepers of hibiscus – Java – red flowers – Power – upon the outer dome of the Mother's Pavilion. There will be rockeries, in Japanese style, with varieties of cactus, small waterfalls, small pools with lilies, marble statues, marble fountains and pavements decorated with precious stones.

The Park of Unity will be divided into twelve gardens, which will represent the twelve attributes of the Supreme Mother. In these gardens I would like to have various kinds of flowers – especially the different types of hibiscus – the Divine Consciousness.

On the other side, towards the boundary of the gardens, I wish to have huge trees like palms, varieties of ferns, neem, Indian cork-trees, eucalyptus and many other beautiful big trees – they all represent unity and aspiration.

Matrimandir: Love.

The twelve gardens: Existence, Consciousness, Bliss, Light, Life, Power, Wealth, Utility, Progress, Youth, Harmony, Perfection.

Banyan tree: Unity.

The park of Unity must be surrounded by a kind of isolating zone so that it is solitary and silent. One has access to it only with permission.

It must be a thing of great beauty – of such a beauty that when men enter the gardens, they will say, 'Ah! This is it!', and experience physically, concretely, the significance of each garden. In the garden of Youth they will know youth; in the garden of Felicity they will know felicity, in the garden of Perfection they will know perfection, and so on. One must know how to move from consciousness to consciousness.

The Mother

The Park of Unity

The dimenstions of the Park of Unity are exactly ten
times those of the structure of Matrimandir: the sphere
36m diameter, height 29m; the oval dimensions 360m
and 290m.

The 12 Gardens:

Existence	A
Consciousness	B
Bliss	C
Light	D
Life	E
Power	F
Wealth	G
Utility	H
Progress	I
Youth	J
Harmony	K
Perfection	L

The 12 Petals:

Sincerity	1
Humility	2
Gratitude	3
Perseverence	4
Aspiration	5
Receptivity	6
Progress	7
Courage	8
Goodness	9
Generosity	10
Equality	11
Peace	12

"The Park of Unity must be surrounded by some kind of isolating zone so that it is solitary and silent. One has access to it only with permission." 1965

"It has been decided and remains decided that the Matrimandir will be surrounded with water. However, water is not available just now and will be available only later; so, it is decided to build the Matrimandir now and surround it with water only later, perhaps in a few years time… The Matrimandir will be built now and water brought around it later." 1970

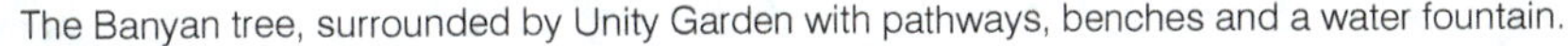

The Banyan tree, surrounded by Unity Garden with pathways, benches and a water fountain.

The biggest difficulty is water, because there is no nearby river up there; but they are already trying to harness rivers. There is even a project to divert water from the Himalayas and bring it across the whole of India ([name] had made a plan and discussed it in Delhi; of course, they objected that it would be a little costly!). But anyway, without going into such grandiose things, something has to be done to bring water; that will be the biggest difficulty, that's what will take the longest time. As for the rest – light, power – it will be made on the spot in the industrial section – but you can't manufacture water!

The Americans have given serious thought to water, because the earth no longer has enough drinking water for people (the water they call fresh... it's ironical); the amount of water is insufficient for people's use, so they have already started chemical experiments on a big scale to transform sea water and make it usable – obviously that would be the solution to the problem.

But it already exists.

It exists, but not in a sufficient proportion.

Yes, in Israel.

They do it in Israel? They use sea water? Obviously, that would be the solution – the sea is there.

It has to be studied.

Then the water would have to be sent uphill.

23 June 1965

...agriculture with the new methods of irrigation using sea water, and of course desalination of the sea water – but they have found something to convert sea water into drinking water (Mother picks up a brochure beside her). It's French I think, an economical method and it's very interesting. It's in process and if we wait a few more years, they'll have perfected it.

30 August 1969

But obviously what is needed... There are material difficulties: for the islet, water is needed – naturally, otherwise it's not an islet! As far as water goes, it will have to be transformed [i.e. by desalination] – there isn't enough underground water.

There's not enough water?

There's water, but just enough for one or two houses; in short there isn't enough water to create a permanent stream. They would have to convert sea water. In Israel they have found a way to do it economically (we even have brochures about it), but you understand, "economical" for a city, not for an individual! And so we have to get water in order to make this islet, that's the difficulty.

30 December 1969

A two-dimensional geometrically formed garden space, a first trial by architects and landscape designers to create the gardens of Existence (on right), Consciousness and Bliss; the best view is from above, here from the top of the Matrimandir.

Gardens of Existence (left & right) and Consciousness (below).

152

Creating a contemplative garden

Martin Mosko is a garden designer who founded the landscape design firm Marpa Design Studio in 1974, and who has won many awards for his work. He is also a Zen monk and Abbot of a Zen temple in Colorado. He recently visited Auroville, during which time he worked with the Matrimandir Gardens design team and gave a public presentation on landscape as sacred space.

Auroville Today (AVT): What kind of garden design do you specialize in?

Martin Mosko (MM): There are many different types of gardens, depending upon the different intention that a garden is trying to express. I limit my work to what I call 'contemplative gardens', or creating sacred spaces.

AVT: How would you define the contemplative garden?

MM: It's a mandala, meaning an energetic system that brings some sense of intentionality rather than chaos, and which is contained by a boundary. It's a seamless integration of many elements into a whole. As such, it expresses harmony and 'atonement' with its environment and culture and its place in time while enhancing certain qualities, like the divine within you. I want my gardens to restore that sense of wholeness, of not being cut off from the world: you become the bird that is singing, the sun setting, the breeze blowing...

AVT: How do you design such a garden?

MM: You can only design such a garden from a contemplative mind: you cannot create it through a logical method.

A good design is always heartfelt, so when I design such a garden I first ask myself, what kind of feeling am I trying to stabilize here? Then, and this is the most difficult part, I need to experience this feeling so deeply in myself that I am completely saturated by it. Once the feeling is stabilized and I empty myself of all preconceptions, the garden comes as a totality, the images just emerge. Then it's just a matter of zooming in to see the details.

AVT: To what extent is the garden related to the client? Do you have to know the client before planning their garden?

MM: It's definitely related to the client. When people call for an architect, they generally want somebody to elegantly display their ego: when they call for a garden designer, they want someone who can express their soul. People don't know how to talk about that, so I have to listen for their deeper aspiration. However, while you can make a garden which is compatible energetically with the client, it must also harmonize with its environment and with itself.

AVT: Do you see in the design of the Matrimandir Gardens elements of the fundamental language of garden design that you spoke about in your talk?

MM: Yes, I do. I think anybody who moves through them is moved by some feeling of what their intention is. At the same time, it's a very particular design. It has nothing to do, for example, with the design of Japanese gardens.

AVT: Would you call the Matrimandir Gardens contemplative gardens?

MM: No, they are not contemplative gardens, nor are they meant to be. A contemplative garden would have trees, it would provide a comfortable way of passing through it and of being able to experience things there. You cannot linger in the Matrimandir Gardens because it is too hot. What you are creating there are jewel boxes, like a necklace around the Matrimandir. I would define them as artworks, three-dimensional artworks which use plant materials and landscaping to express a particular quality or qualities that have been defined by The Mother.

A contemplative garden starts from integration. If I was to design the Matrimandir area, I would have started with the Lake and the way the Lake relates to the land and the community. Then I would have seen how the gardens fitted into that and only then would I have decided on the location of the Matrimandir.

To me the contemplative garden resembles the Japanese and Chinese vision of a complete seamless integration of man and nature, where nature penetrates everything and is the dominant factor: this creates the harmony that I look for as a garden designer. The Western model of architecture and garden design is the opposite of this; it expresses the domination of man over nature.

AVT: Which model do you sense is predominant in Auroville?

MM: In the past, Aurovilians put a lot of good energy into the land: it's a magnificent achievement. However, I think it would be a good idea to reinvigorate that energy now because I think that awareness is getting neglected. As a humble outsider, I would suggest that any proposal for a building project should first be reviewed by gardeners and landscape designers; that the land and the environment be considered before the architects are brought into the team. Then there should be a sensible integration of gardens and architecture to create a unity which is harmonious and sustainable. This is an approach that begins with the container, the whole, which is the garden space, the sacred space. I think that awareness is lacking at the moment.

What I also see a need for around here is small gathering spaces and a way of getting you from place to place that is enjoyable, that, instead of speeding you up, slows you down, bringing you more into the present. And nothing slows you down better than beauty...

AVT: What is your impression of the gardens you have visited in Auroville?

MM: There are a lot of interesting gardens here. I went to Gaia's Garden for the tea ceremony and that's a beautiful garden, and I went to a really nice garden at Afsaneh's place. A lot of people have a really good feeling for gardens. Take Marco's garden. Here is an example of someone who started with the garden. Here is an example of someone whose garden co-evolved with his house. That's why it feels really comfortable there. In fact, a famous feng shui master told him that his house had the best feng shui of any house in Auroville. Feng shui is an innate ability in all of us if we pay attention to things with a view of the whole rather than just trying to accomplish a need which is on our mind at that moment.

It's all about finding the right balance, and an awareness that balance begins with the garden and with seeing things whole. From my point of view, the Earth is a garden, and we should look at it like that and treat it like that. But we should view even a small garden as a whole in itself while being related to larger wholes like the surrounding environment and the specific culture in which it is located.

If we follow this approach, we can recreate a world which is sustainable and spiritually uplifting. This is the feeling that always happens in a garden: you feel uplifted.

Harvesting rainwater for Auroville's water needs

Groundwater

Groundwater is the only drinking water resource that Auroville and the surrounding population uses today. But the resource is extremely fragile. Already in 1996, French scientists warned that the aquifers underneath the Auroville region will turn saline. "We know from recent government data that the situation around Auroville has deteriorated and that seawater is already beginning to intrude into the aquifers," says Gilles. "We are sitting on a time-bomb. When it happens, it will be sudden rather than gradual. Then, 400,000 people in our bioregion will be affected."

"The bunds and check-dams that Auroville created have a positive effect on the aquifer," says Gilles. "They ensure that rainwater percolates into the aquifer, which benefits the villages. Auroville benefits indirectly as the recharge augments the groundwater volume and so delays saline water intruding into the aquifer. But it will not prevent it. We are in the danger area. Auroville's work is commendable; but if we look at the total area, Auroville's environmental impact is no more than 1%." For Auroville, we have to look at different options."

Creating the lake in Sadhana Forest

Rainwater harvesting

One of these options is rainwater harvesting. "It's nothing new," says Gilles. "The ancient Tamil kings created a whole interconnected system of erys and lakes which got filled with rainwater. This water was then used for agriculture. "For the urban areas, too, the ancient kings developed rainwater harvesting structures. But during the last centuries the approach has changed to trying to get rid of rainwater as fast as possible. Rainwater is considered a nuisance rather than a potential resource. Then, paradoxically, gigantic efforts are undertaken to bring water back to the very same urban areas, often from far away and at tremendous cost."

In Auroville, rainwater harvesting is only being done to recharge the aquifer (with the exception of Annapurna and Ayarpadi Farm which use it also for irrigation). "But we found that rainwater harvesting can be one of the major water resources for the city," says Gilles. This, he says, would require one or more storage tanks with a total capacity of 300,000 cubic metres. "The design for capturing and storing rainwater needs to be planned and integrated within the city layout," says Gilles. "It means that drainage conduits and rainwater capturing zones will have to be designed as part of the urban landscape, using existing topographic features. We propose that a network of natural waterways is created all over Auroville which would drain the rainwater into the storage areas This could

Pond in the International House area

Bunding in the International Zone area

lead to a very nice urban landscape, where the waterways would be filled up during monsoons and be empty during the rest of the year. As rainwater is prone to pollution, these waterways would help in the cleaning process through appropriate designs, landscape and vegetation. A final water treatment system would cleanse the water before it would be fed into the drinking water supply."

Multi-sourcing

Though rainwater harvesting can be the major water source, the study does not recommend relying solely on it. Instead it proposes using a combination of resources.

"This," says Gilles, "has a lot of advantages. It makes the system very sturdy and allows for flexibility to keep pace with the population growth; there is no need to invest in systems which are meant for a much larger population.

"So a multi-sourcing strategy is essential. Based on a population model of 15,000 people, a combination of resources has been examined. Our technical and economic evaluation shows that fresh groundwater is the cheapest source, followed by harvested rainwater, then desalinized brackish groundwater, while desalinized seawater is the most expensive. Taking into account the investment and running costs over a 20-year period, a mix of rainwater harvesting, desalination of brackish water and a back-up of groundwater – e.g. extracted from pockets of ground water that are not threatened by seawater intrusion and which can be recharged and maintained – will be the most feasible solution to achieve water security for Auroville.

"Tim Rees, an early Aurovilian who made the first hydrological study of Auroville, told us that Mother said to him in 1972 that there is enough water and that the Aurovilians will have to use their ingenuity to collect it and make use of it. That's what we are trying to do."

Auroville bioregion

The Auroville bioregion is part of the Kaluveli coastal watershed, which covers about 762 square kilometres (76,200 ha.). This watershed is located in the Tindivanam and Vanur blocks between Marakanam, Tindivanam and Pondicherry towns and drains into the Kaluveli tank, which has a single outlet to the sea near Marakanam. The eastern boundary runs for about 35 kms along the Bay of Bengal between Marakanam and Pondicherry.

The Kaluveli tank is a seasonal lake and is one of the last unpolluted water bodies of South India. It is also an important wintering place for migrating water birds, with more than 100 different species recorded.

The region is primarily devoted to agriculture, with the main crops being rice, sugar cane and coconut, along with lesser amounts of vegetables for local consumption. There are also tree plantations, including recently introduced cashew orchards, planted stands of casuarinas used for firewood, and a few stands of older indigenous trees, mostly in protected groves associated with religious sites. A major issue is the recent development of shrimp farms in the tank, often without permits or proper controls. Although these provide income, they also introduce pollutants into the Kaluveli lake, from where they enter the groundwater.

Due to its unique physical conditions, it has been suggested that the region be declared a Biosphere Reserve under the UNESCO Man and Biosphere Program (MAB). Although no action on this proposal has

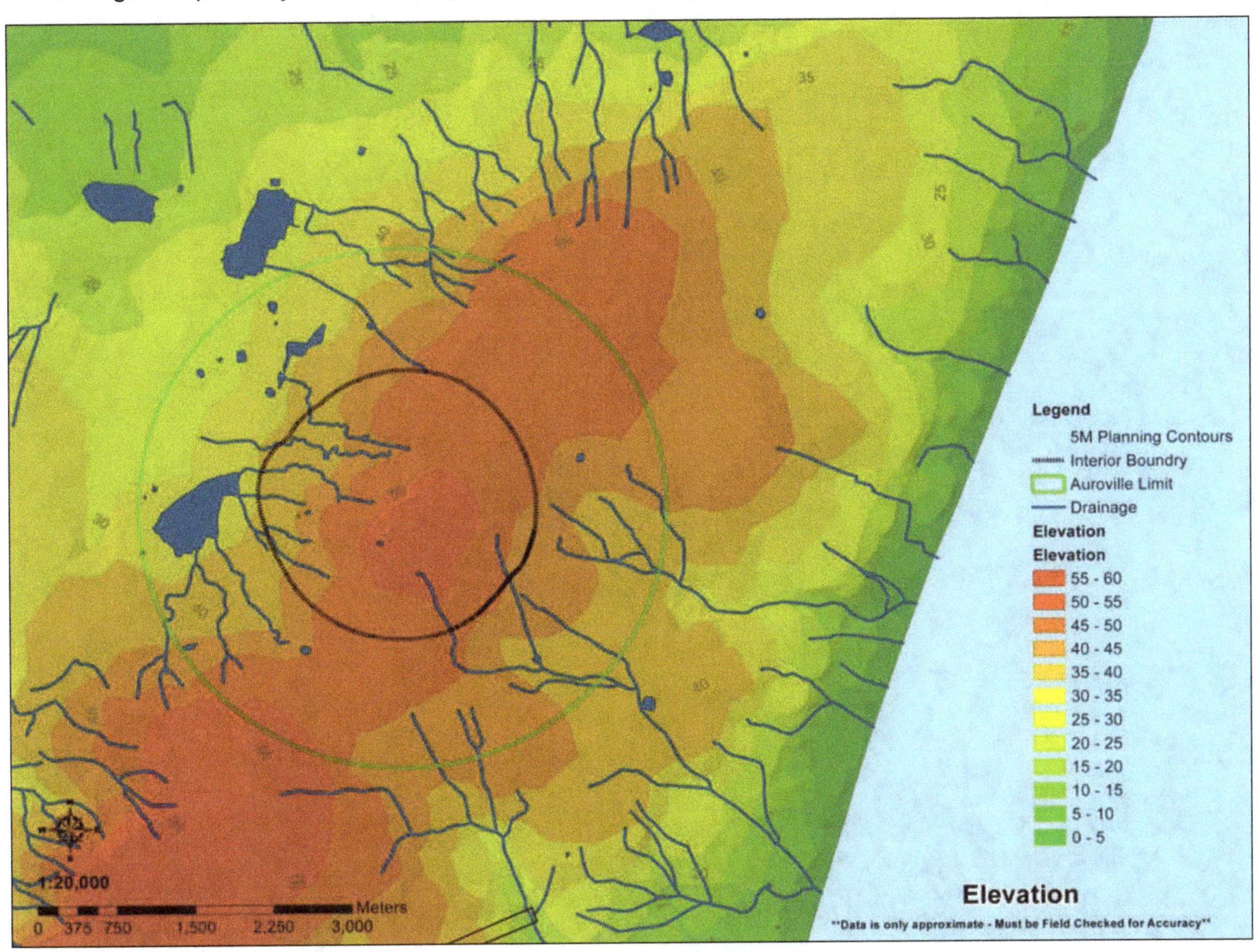

yet been taken, it does indicate that there is a degree of recognition of the threats to its long term viability, and the need to undertake protective and remedial action. The programme for the Auroville Green Belt is one contribution in this direction, and it is to be hoped that it will encourage a wider understanding of the issues and methods of addressing them within the bioregion, the state of Tamil Nadu and the Union Territory of Puducherry.

Physically, the bioregion consists of a narrow coastal plain, a slight rise running parallel to the coast, reaching an elevation of 50 metres at the location of the Matrimandir in Auroville, and then a slope downward toward the west from this low ridge toward the Kaluveli tank.

During the monsoons, a substantial amount of water drains into the Kaluveli tank, and then ultimately into the sea.

Water in the bioregion

All of the streams and rivers in the area are seasonal, flowing only during the monsoons, and becoming dry during other seasons. Surface water storage structures, including irrigation tanks and ponds, provide the major source of stored water in the bioregion. Auroville has initiated and actively participated in a number of efforts to restore tanks in the region.

Overall, one may attribute the poor level of groundwater recharge to several factors, including the

severe erosion of the land, which has become gullied in many locations; the loss of arable soil to retain water both within the soil itself and to support the vegetation that slows water movement; and seriously diminished biodiversity. These are the main factors that have lead to poor groundwater recharge.

The region receives rain during two periods, the south-west monsoon from July to September, and the north-east monsoon from October to December. The north-east monsoon also generates periodic cyclones as it moves across the Bay of Bengal, the most recent being Cyclone Thane, which caused very substantial damage to homes, farms and trees throughout the bioregion.

During the rains, and in particular during the second or north-east monsoon, runoff exceeds the capacity of many of the channels and ponds. This has resulted in additional erosion, deepening the gullies, as well as the discharge of a substantial amount of fresh water directly into the sea, since the capacity of the ponds and tanks is insufficient to retain the volume.

The water table in certain layers of the aquifer nearer the coast now lies below sea level (MSL) and seawater has started to intrude in these sectors. In some areas, this intrusion has already reached as far as 8 km inland, thus threatening the main source of drinking water for the entire region. New technologies (such as rotary drilling rigs, submersible pumps, etc.), have enabled farmers to draw water from deeper aquifers. These farmers are also supplied with free electricity by the Tamil Nadu Electricity Board (TNEB). This has resulted in pumping without

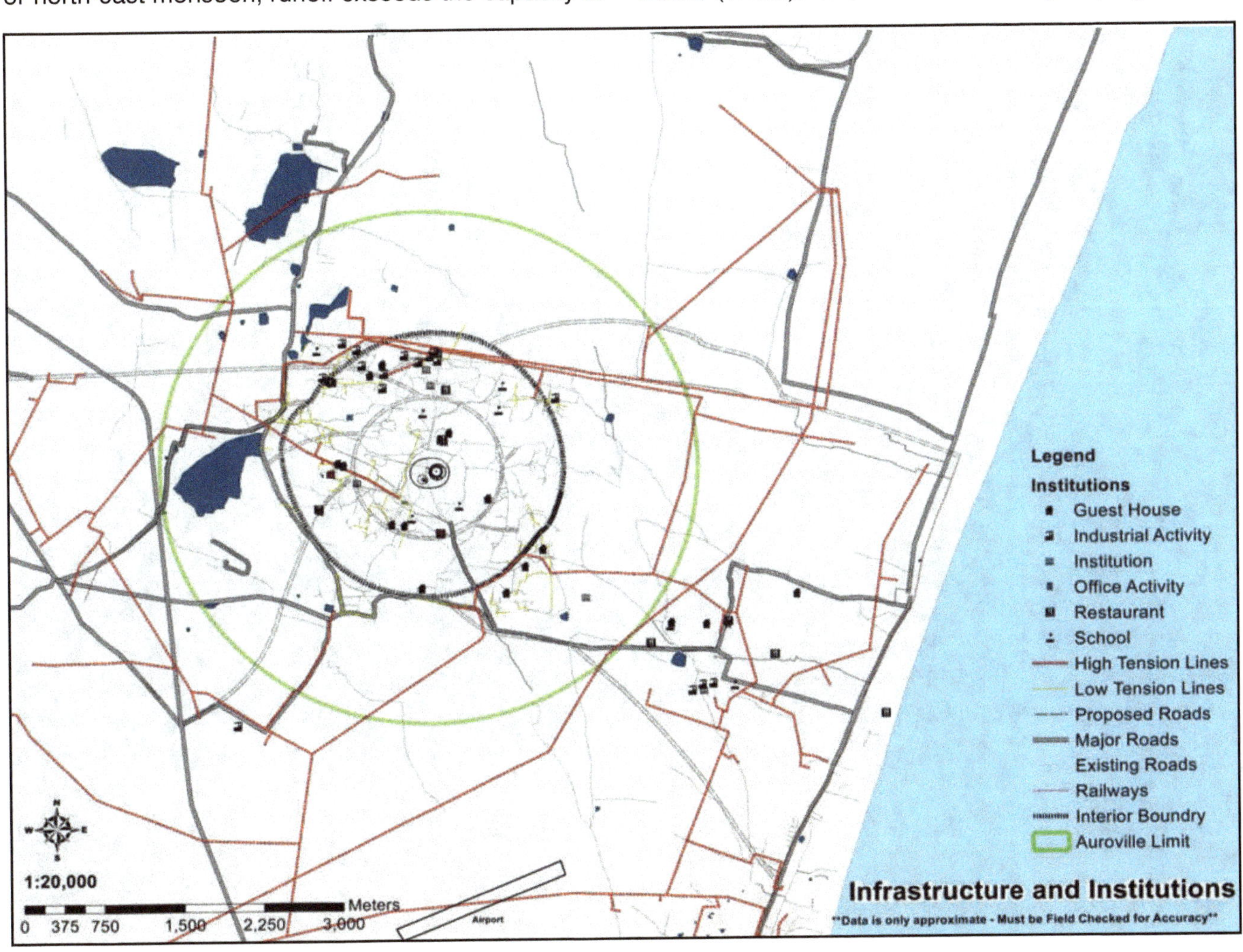

restriction round the clock, thus extracting massive (and unused) amounts of groundwater.

Many farmers, lacking an understanding of the consequences, use excessive amounts of fertilizers and pesticides. This has resulted in polluted runoff which then enters the groundwater. Recent analyses have shown a serious increase of pesticide load in the water. Another pollutant is salt from sea water intrusion, which initially began in the south of Kaluveli tank, and now shows an impact on groundwater quality in much of the bioregion.

The receding availability of water will affect the entire population of the coastal area by depriving them of a secure supply of safe drinking water. It will also affect interior towns that are pumping their drinking water. Farmers will be severely affected in the absence of suitable irrigation water to meet their requirements, creating a looming catastrophe with very wide implications on the political and social stability of the entire region.

The Green Belt

The Green Belt is a patchwork of wooded areas, agriculture, streams, ponds and human habitation covering some 15 sq.kms. The initial plan designated a circle surrounding the town. While there is a defined legal boundary to the Green Belt, at the moment there is no physical distinction that would identify lands

which lie within or outside. At present, Auroville owns, through the Auroville Foundation, about a quarter of the land within the Green Belt. This land is managed with special attention to sustainable practices. Increasing land prices have begun to encourage developers and speculators to bid up the price of land in areas which are becoming more accessible in the immediate vicinity of Auroville, especially along the East Coast Road (ECR) and the new Bypass Highway. The vegetation of the Green Belt is a mixture of both exotic and indigenous flora, forming restored and native woodlands, tree plantations, orchards and crop production land, together with vacant, often barren areas. Informally, much of the accessible open space is used for passive recreation.

Present agricultural production in the Green Belt involves the growing of coconuts, sugar cane, rice, cashews and fruit trees such as papaya, mango and banana. In addition some farmers cultivate vegetables and medicinal herbs, or plant casuarina trees.

Two paved rural roads serve vehicular traffic, running between the ECR and the bypass through the villages of Edayanchavadi and Alankuppam. Internally, gravel and dirt roads and paths crisscross the entire area, and one paved road, the Auroville Crown Road, has been partially constructed. These provide access to animals and uncontrolled grazing on the open space, as well as unrestricted use by wheeled vehicles.

Water

Auroville is located at the highest point of the Kaluveli basin, along the ridge that divides the drainage between the basin and the Bay of Bengal. A portion flows east in seasonal streams and is stored in basins behind check-dams; its percolation goes fast and it recharges the aquifers. Most of the rest flows west and then north to Kaluveli. A smaller portion flows to the south, feeding the streams flowing into Pondicherry, The streams feed two large erys or tanks, located in Irumbai and Alankuppam. With rainfall between 1,200 and 1,500 mm per year, and the generally flat character of the land, proper management can make a substantial portion of the rainfall percolate back into the ground. Water management efforts

within Auroville have been a significant contributor to the improvement of local conditions, enhancing the recharge that supplies some 190 wells throughout the town and Green Belt. However, as noted in the discussion above, the fact that these aquifers are not limited to Auroville, but underlie the entire bioregion, means that over-pumping elsewhere in the aquifer jeopardizes the supply for all, including Auroville. In fact, because Auroville lies at the apex, it is in some ways more vulnerable.

In order to maximize its contribution to the recharge, Auroville has developed a large number of bunds and check-dams to slow runoff and allow more water to enter the ground, both on the west and on the east of the ridge. In normal monsoons Auroville has hardly any runoff. Auroville is become a sponge. Where check-dams

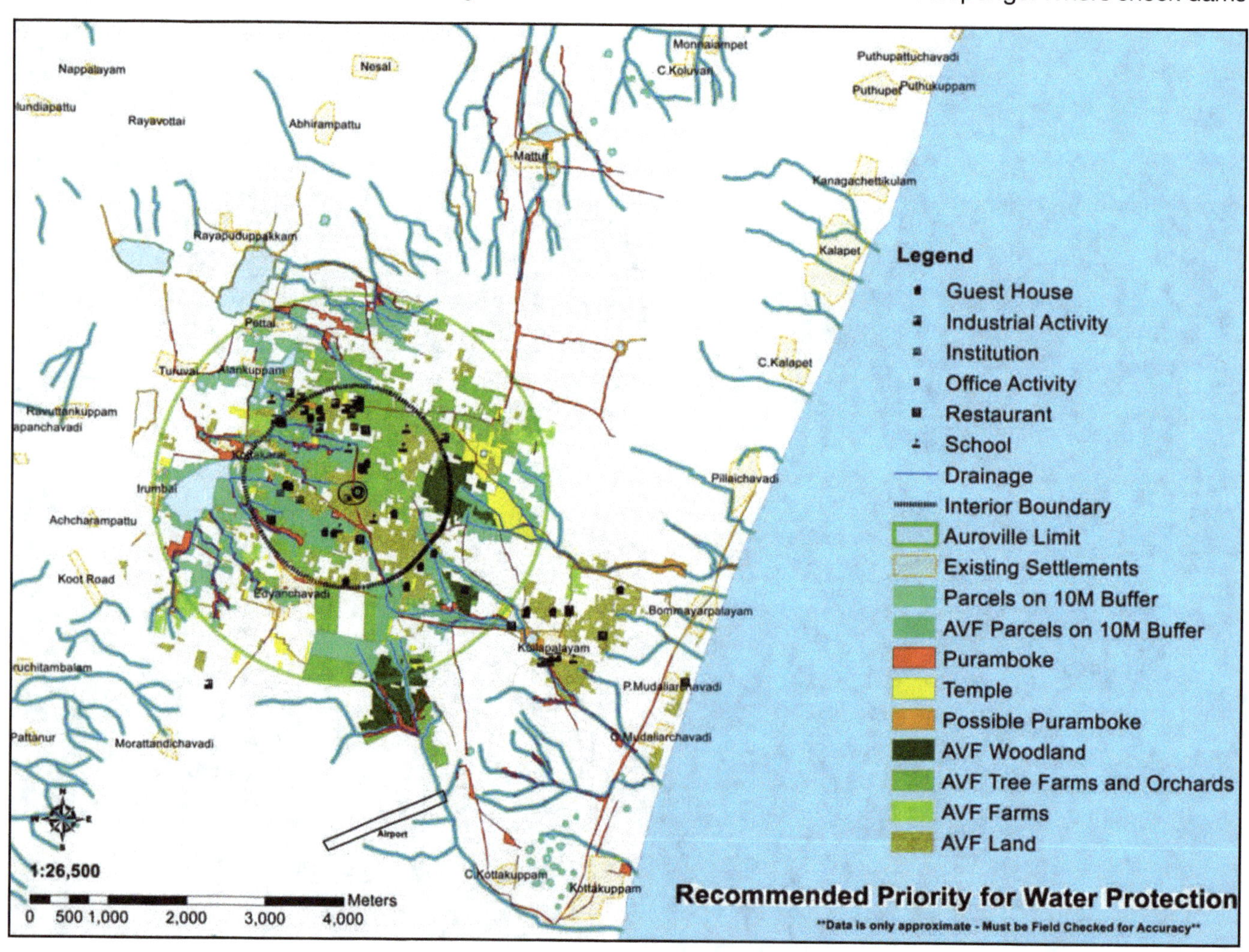

have been built and water basins created the vegetation came back spontaneously. The canyons are now green and very much alive. However there is a tendency to turn the canyons into roads as the runoff is nearly nil in normal monsoons. There are two stream systems that flow east from within the Green Belt into Kuilapalayam and Bommayapalayam and one that flows south-east from the area of Forecomers toward Pondicherry Airport. These are highly vulnerable to urban encroachment and loss of function. The lack of active management along much of the length of two of these (those flowing through Kuilapalayam panchayat) substantially increases the amount of waste and pollution that is allowed to accumulate and enter the ground along their lengths.

Two streams that drain into the Irumbai Tank come from the International Zone. Here most of the water percolates behind bunds and a systems of ponds. The last is a tank of 15.000 m³ in Ayarpadi Farm, meant for rice crops.

"The International Zone forms a small part, about 26%, of the total drainage area of the Irumbai Lake," says water expert Gilles Boulicot. "Nowadays, the Lake is less in use for irrigation; the villagers rather work with borewells. So they will benefit from Kireet's work, as there will be more water going into the aquifers. There will be no adverse effect for the villages."

Farmers in Auroville have noted that water for irrigation is a matter of serious mid-term and long-term concern. They have developed and implemented many water saving technologies, and have successfully demonstrated that crops can be profitably grown

with far less water than is currently the common practice in the wider bioregion. But the continuance of over-pumping elsewhere from the aquifers puts the entire region at risk for the loss of both domestic and agricultural supplies, and needs to be addressed urgently.

Green Belt Plan

The Green Belt Plan focuses on the primary concern of the region, which is the preservation and protection of the water supply for Auroville and its surroundings through the supervision and maintenance of the area gazetted as the Green Belt. The water source for Auroville is part of a larger aquifer that supports nearly 350,000 residents in the Kaluveli Basin. Thus, it has been necessary to not only respond to the Auroville area located in the Green Belt itself, but to demonstrate the inseparable connections to the wider bioregion and, therefore, to propose a plan that is intended as the first stage of a larger, regional effort.

The Green Belt Plan is the first major revision of the Master Plan. This plan does not seek to specify uses for each individual piece of land, since adequate data is not currently available. Rather, it outlines the areas that are most appropriate for protection under four categories – water management, woodlands and tree plantations, farms, and recreation. The plan suggests where the emphasis needs to be placed on controlling land uses, especially with regard to the protection and conservation of these areas, together with an indication

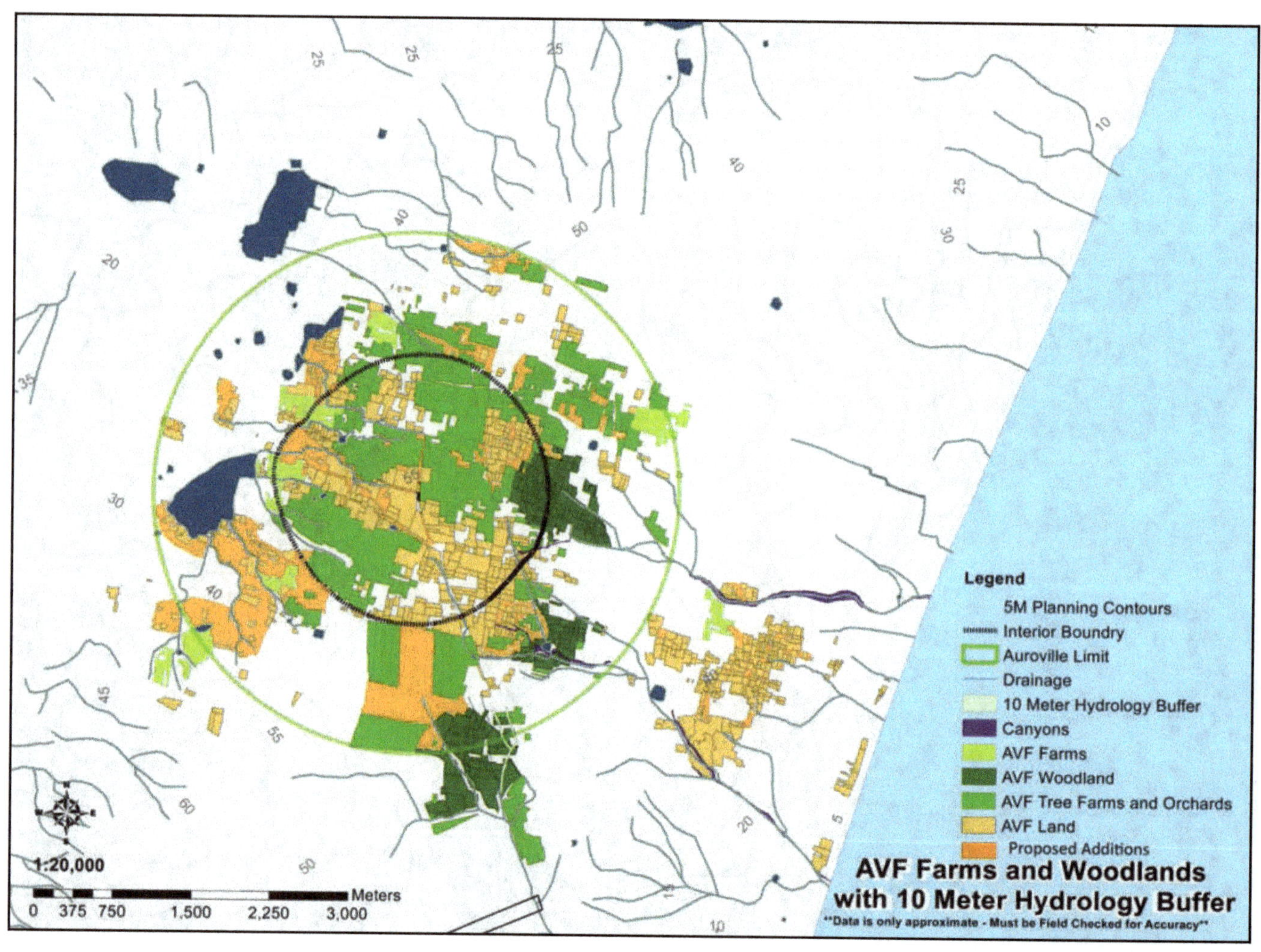

of the priorities for the further acquisition of land within the Green Belt as opportunities arise.

The initial designation of the Green Belt was based on a symbolic image of the township, formed by two concentric circles of 1.25 and 2.5 km diameter, centred on the Banyan tree by the Matrimandir.

This plan, after much consideration, modifies this approach, and instead seeks to propose modifications to the Green Belt in order to more accurately reflect its functions. This will make it easier to maintain the Green Belt and provides the rationale for its continued development and expansion, since it is technically consistent with both the reality of the location and with the accepted practices of planning and administration.

Because Auroville only controls a limited portion of the critical areas, the plan distinguishes between those areas for which Auroville has direct responsibility, namely the area within the boundary gazetted by the Government of India, and the areas outside, which need to be managed through a cooperative arrangement with authorities in the wider bioregion.

The first task for this plan dealt with the re-drawing of the original boundaries of the Green Belt.

The boundary of the Green Belt, because of the central role which it plays in the protection of water resources, should be adjusted to extend beyond the present boundary of the Green Belt in a number of circumstances. It is therefore recommended that Auroville seek to formally adjust the boundary to include

Section of the new Crown Road passing through the Green Belt

the full parcel for every parcel that the symbolic circle passes through. It is also recommended that protection be extended to include a 10m. buffer on each side of all water bodies and water courses throughout the bioregion, and in particular for those water courses flowing directly into the Bay of Bengal on the east side of Auroville, where the first impacts of saltwater intrusion will be felt.

The first priority consists of those portions of the ephemeral streams running through the canyons, together with all water bodies which directly aid in the process of the aquifer recharge. These need to be treated in a unitary manner covering their entire length, especially those areas which are integral parts of the Kaluveli basin

Woodlands

The story of Auroville is the story of a near miracle – the small band of settlers starting in 1968 who began planting trees on a barren tableland north of Pondicherry. Over the years, around 2 million trees have been planted, and the area has changed from being in an advanced state of desertification to a lush environment with a great variety of trees that have not only revived the soil, but have brought back wildlife, improved the climate, and provided livelihood for thousands. Initial plantings concentrated on just stabilizing the soil, including many exotic species such as eucalyptus and acacia. As these took hold, more recent efforts have focused on re-creating the so-called Tropical Dry Evergreen Forest or TDEF, and replacing ageing exotic trees with species more suited to the climate and conditions of south India.

Vision and issues

The Green Belt Plan has four main purposes:

1. To delineate common objectives and policies for the maintenance and management of the complex entity termed the Green Belt.

2. To help establish a clearer direction and process for the conservation and rehabilitation management of the land around the entire water system serving Auroville.

3. To aid the development of good relationships between the Auroville communities in the bioregion and in particular the villages adjoining Auroville, other landowners, and special interest groups, with respect to management and enhancement of the land designated as the green corridors, buffers and patches.

4. To establish tools and methods for determining appropriate uses of privately owned land within the Green Belt, and for working with owners to ensure that any development is consistent with the intentions of the Master Plan.

Recognize the special relationship between Auroville and the villages lying partly within the Green Belt.

There are critical common needs which are shared by the entire population of the Auroville area, which necessitate direct links and mechanisms for sharing resources, knowledge and skills for the common benefit of all.
The Plan encourages village authorities to exercise their responsibilities, as well as to fulfill their aspirations for active involvement in the management of this bioregion in partnership with Auroville. The Plan provides guidance by which each of them may manage lands within their jurisdiction while respecting and reflecting the distinctive landscapes of Auroville and the bioregion, which are a mix of natural and human influences. The Plan also recognizes the nature of the changes and growth of the human population, and thus the inevitability that some changes will occur and need to be balanced by a shared commitment to maintain the green infrastructure to the maximum degree possible.

Auroville Today

The function of the Matrimandir lake

"In our study we took in the Matrimandir lake," says Gilles. "The lake, which surrounds the Matrimandir and its inner gardens, has a symbolic and aesthetic value. We studied the ways and potential to sustain the lake in its three functions: aesthetic, symbolic and practical e.g. to what extent it is possible to use it as part of the Auroville rainwater harvesting network. We then found that the lake has never been well planned. The surrounding buildings, such as the Town Hall, which were created about ten years ago, are situated about two metres below the planned lake level. We calculated to see if harvested rainwater could be used to fill the lake, and afterwards maintain its water level when there is leakage and evaporation. We found it cannot. The topography around the lake is such that one part is lower and another higher than the lake. The only rainwater that can be harvested is from the latter area and from the Matrimandir's inner gardens. But that run-off would be insufficient to compensate for the losses, even with a lake level fluctuation of 75 centimetres as allowed by late Chief Architect Roger Anger. Additionally, there would be no possibility to use the lake as part of the rainwater harvesting network.

"To solve the problem you can either redesign the topography – which means a lot of earth movement – or use the existing topography. We chose the latter option and explored the potential of designing a 'step-lake' or a 'terraced lake' like the rice fields in Bali, so that there is a much larger area which can drain into it. Such a lake would have three to four levels or more, with 50-100 centimetre steps, each proportional to the corresponding drainage catchment area. It could be very beautiful. The aesthetic aspect of such a lake could include waterfalls and moving water and the design could integrate the already grown-up trees around Matrimandir on islands. In this way the lake can be maintained naturally from an effective drainage area of 1,446,000m2 (356 acres) bordering Matrimandir.

"Such a drainage area, however, will at times provide more water than the lake can store. So there will be a very large overflow which will need to be stored in a secondary reservoir, which can be emptied as required. We calculated that this reservoir, with a capacity of 150,000 cubic metres (or a surface area of 30,000 square metres of 5 metre depth), would not only be useful to help maintain the levels of the lake in the dry season, but also in combination with Matrimandir lake be able to supply a population of 15,000 people for, on average, 220 days a year." The calculation, he explains, is made on the basis of a projected consumption of 107 litres per capita per day (lcd), which is less than half the 270 lcd as indicated in the Indian National Building Code.

A schematic view of the Auroville energy and water scenario. Wind generators feed into the grid, which feeds residences, the desalination plant and the pumping station. Desalinated water is fed into the Auroville drinking water supply system and the Matrimandir Lake.

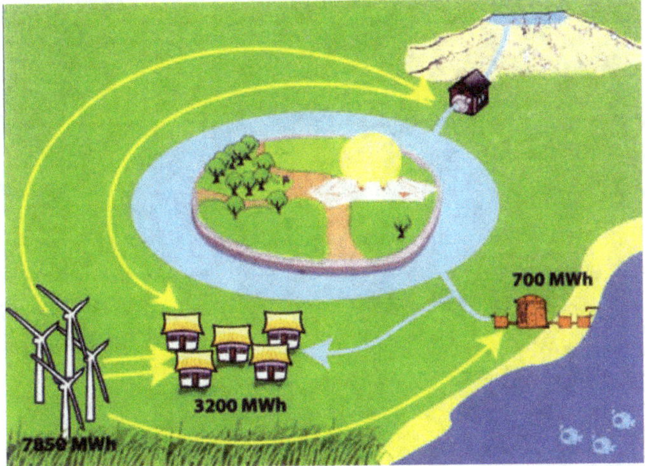

Contact details

General information on Auroville:
info@auroville.org.in

Public/media relations:
outreachmedia@auroville.org.in

Auroville International website:
www.auroville-international.org

Auroville website:
www.auroville.org

Other publications

Auroville Architecture
towards new forms for a new consciousness

Auroville Form Style and Design
towards new forms for a new consciousness

Acknowledgements

Photographs:

Major contributors: John Mandeen
Franz Fassbender

Other photos:
Barun Tagore, pp. 18-21,24,28-29,42,43,44(Top)
Anita, pp. 35,40,41,45,48
Dominique Darr, pp. 6,7,8,9,10 (Top),11
Giorgio Molinari, pp. 61,62,63,64,65, 94, 95

We also thank Auroville Archives for making it
possible to use photos of Auroville's early years.

The texts by Sri Aurobindo and the Mother
are copyright of the Sri Aurobindo Ashram
Trust, Pondicherry, and are reproduced
here with acknowledgement and
thanks to the Trustees.
The copyright holder for Mother's Agenda is
"Institut de Recherches Evolutives", Paris.

Designed and produced by:

PRISMA, Aurelec-Prayogashala
Auroville 605101, Tamil Nadu, INDIA
prisma@auroville.org.in
Tel: +91-413-2622296
Fax: +91-413-2622185

Concept & Layout: Franz Fassbender
D.T.P. work: S. Janarthanan

© PRISMA
ISBN 978-81-928152-2-0
First edition: 2013

Printed at:
Sudarsan Graphics, Chennai, INDIA

Text:

pp. 6-7	The Mother, 10th July 1957
pp. 12-17	Equals One The Journal of Auroville City, 1968
pp. 22-23	Mother's Agenda 3rd February, 1968, Vol.9, pp.41-42
pp. 24-25	Auroville Today, by Alan, February 2003, No.169
pp. 26	Mother's Agenda 3rd February, 1968, Vol.9, pp.41-42
pp. 28-29	Mother's Agenda 28 February 1968, Vol.9, pp.66-70
pp. 32-33	Equals One Experiment Auroville, pp.78-79
pp. 36-39	Legend of Irumbai Temple The Spirit of Auroville, pp 30-32
pp. 44-48	Turning Points, An inner story of the beginnings of Auroville, Auroville Press Publishers, 2008
pp. 50-52	Kireet (Gerard Jak)
pp. 58-60	Auroville Architects Monograph Series, Poppo Pingel, by Mona Doctor-Pingel, Mapin Publishing, 2012
pp. 62-63	Auroville's afforestation The Auroville Adventure, July 1989
pp. 68-69	Gardens in Auroville, Auroville Today, February 2010, No. 252
pp. 112-114	Zen gardens, Auroville Today, February 2010, No. 252
p. 130	Auroville Today, September 2007, No. 223
pp.140-141	The Mother Auroville References in Mother's Agenda
pp.144-145	The Flowers of Auroville Sri Aurobindo's Action, June 2010
pp.146-147	Quotations from Mother's Agenda
p.150-151	23 June 1965, MA VI-139-150 30 August 1969, MA X-333-336 30 December 1969, MA X-525-536
pp.154-155	Auroville Today, April 2012, No. 273
pp.156-158	Auroville Today, March 2013, No. 284
pp.159-168	Auroville Today, September 2012, No. 278
p.168	Auroville Today, February 2012, No. 270

International Publications

Auroville Architecture
by Franz Fassbender

Auroville Form Style and Design
by Franz Fassbender

Landscapes and Gardens of Auroville
by Franz Fassbender

Inauguration of Auroville
by Franz Fassbender

Auroville in a Nutshell
by Tim Wrey

Death doesn't exist
The Mother on Death, Sri Aurobindo on Rebirth
Compiled by Franz Fassbender

Divine Love
Compiled by Franz Fassbender

Five Dream
by Sri Aurobindo

Vision
Compiled by Franz Fassbender

Passage to More than India
by Dick Batstone

The Mother on Japan
Compiled by Franz Fassbender

Children of Change: A Spiritual Pilgrimage
by Amrit (Howard Shoji Iriyama)

Memories of Auroville - told by early Aurovilians
by Janet Feran

The Journeying Years
by Dianna Bowler

Auroville Reflected
by Bindu Mohanty

Finding the Psychic Being
by Loretta Shartsis

The Teachings of Flowers
The Life and Work of the Mother of the Sri Aurobindo Ashram
by Loretta Shartsis

The Supramental Transformation
by Loretta Shartsis

The Mother's Yoga - 1956-1973 (English & Frech)
Vol. 1, 1956-1967 & Vol. 2, 1968-1973
by Loretta Shartsis

Antithesis of Yoga
by Jocelyn Janaka

Bougainvilleas PROTECTION
by Narad (Richard Eggenberger), Nilisha Mehta

Crossroad The New Humanity
by Paulette Hadnagy

Die Praxis Des Integralen Yoga
By M. P. Pandit

The Way of the Sunlit Path
William Sullivan

Wildlife great and small of India's Coromandel
by Tim Wrey

A New Education With A Soul
Marguerite Smithwhite

Featured Titles

Divine Love

The texts presented in this book are selected from the Mother and Sri Aurobindo.

"Awakened to the meaning of my heart. That to feel love and oneness is to live. And this the magic of our golden change, is all the truth I know or seek, O sage."

Sri Aurobindo, Savitri, Book XII, Epilog

A Vision by the Mother

On 28th May 1958, the Mother recounted a vision she once had of a wonderful Being of Love and Consciousness, emanated from the Supreme Origin and projected directly into the Inconscient so that the creation would gradually awaken to the Supramental Consciousness. The Mother's account of this vision was brought out a first time in November 1906, in the Revue Cosmique, a monthly review published in Paris.

A Dream – Aims and Ideals of Auroville
the Mother on Auroville

50 years of Auroville from 28.02.1968 - 28.02.2018

Today, information about Auroville is abundant. Many people try to make meaning out of Auroville – about its conception, to what direction should we grow towards, and, what are we doing here?

But what was Mother's original Dream and what was her Vision for Auroville back then?

Matrimandir Talks by the Mother

This book presents most of Mother's Matrimandir talks, including how she conceived the idea for this special concentration and meditation building in Auroville.

Memories of Auroville - Told by early Aurovilians

Memories of Auroville is a book about the very early days of Auroville based on interviews made in 1997 with Aurovilians who lived here between 1968 and 1973. The interviews presented in this book are part of a history program for newcomers that I had created with my friend, Philip Melville in 1997. The plan was to divide Auroville's history into different eras and then interview Aurovilians according to their area of knowledge. Our first section would cover the years from 1968 till 1973 when the Mother was still in her physical body.

The Way of the Sunlit Path

May The Way of the Sunlit Path be a convenient guide for activating this ancient truth as a support for a Conscious Evolution.
May it illumine the transformation offered to us in the Integral Yoga.

A Dream Takes Shape (in English, French, Hindi)

A comprehensive brochure on the international township of Auroville in, ranging from its Charter and "Why Auroville?" to the plan of the township, the central Matrimandir, the national pavilions and residences, to working groups, the economy, making visits, how to join, its relationship to the Sri Aurobindo Ashram, and its key role in the future of the world. This brochure endeavours to highlight how The Mother envisioned Auroville from its inception, some of the major achievements realised over the years, and some of the difficulties currently faced in implementing the guidelines which she gave.

Mother on Japan

I had everything to learn in Japan. For four years, from an artistic point of view, I lived from wonder to wonder. And everything in this city, in this country, from beginning to end, gives you the impression of impermanence, of the unexpected, the exceptional... ...everything in this city, in this country, from beginning to end, gives you the impression of impermanence, of the unexpected, the exceptional. You always come to things you did not expect; you want to find them again and they are lost – they have made something else which is equally charming.

Auroville Reflected

On 28 February 1968, on an impoverished plateau on the Coromandel Coast of South India, about 4,000 people from around the world gathered for a most unusual inauguration. Handfuls of soil from the countries of the world were mixed together as a symbol of human unity. Why did Indira Gandhi, the erstwhile Prime Minister of India, support this development for "a city the earth needs?" Why did UNESCO endorse this project? Why does the Dalai Lama continue to be involved in the project? What led anthropologist Margaret Mead to insist that records must be kept of its progress? Why did both historian William Irwin Thompson and United Nations representative Robert Muller note that this social experiment may be a breakthrough for humanity even as critics commented, "it is an impossible dream"?

A House For the Third Millennium

Essays on Matrimandir

Nightwatch at the Matrimandir...
A cosmic spectacle; the black expanse above, the big black crater of Matrimandir's excavation carved deep into the soil. The four pillars - two of which are completed and the other two nearing completion - are four huge ships coming together from the four corners of the earth to meet at this pro propitious spot...

Passage to More than India

This book is a voyage of discovery. In 1959 the author, Dick Batstone, a classically educated bookseller in England, with a Christian background, comes across a life of the great Indian polymath Sri Aurobindo, though a series of apparently fortuitous circumstances. A meeting in Durham, England, leads him to a determination to get to the Sri Aurobindo Ashram in Pondicherry, a former French territory south of Madras.